CAMBRIDGE SKILLS FOR FLUENCY
Series Editor: Adrian Doff

Reading 3

Simon Greenall
Diana Pye

CAMBRIDGE
UNIVERSITY PRESS

Published by the Press Syndicate of the University of Cambridge
The Pitt Building, Trumpington Street, Cambridge CB2 1RP
40 West 20th Street, New York, NY 10011–4211, USA
10 Stamford Road, Oakleigh, Melbourne 3166, Australia

© Cambridge University Press 1992

First published 1992
Third printing 1996

Printed in Great Britain
by Scotprint Ltd, Musselburgh

ISBN 0 521 34673 8

BH

Contents

Map of the book

Unit	Functions/Structural areas	Vocabulary areas	Reading strategies
1 Lies	Describing routine activities; present simple; making excuses.	Everyday actions.	Predicting; extracting main ideas; understanding the writer's intention.
2 Coincidences	Talking about the past; past simple.	Surprising events.	Predicting; extracting main ideas; dealing with unfamiliar words; reacting to the text.
3 Nightmare journeys	Describing a sequence of actions; present tense for storytelling.	Travel; flying.	Understanding the writer's intention; extracting main ideas; inferring.
4 The cow that ate the piper	Telling a story; past tenses.	Folktales.	Predicting; extracting main ideas; evaluating the text.
5 He was a good lion	Telling a story.	Wildlife.	Extracting main ideas; dealing with unfamiliar words; predicting; evaluating the text.
6 Bargains	Describing routine activities and behaviour; present simple.	Shopping.	Dealing with unfamiliar words; extracting main ideas; reading for specific information; evaluating the text; understanding the writer's style.
7 A lamp in a window	Describing personal behaviour and characteristics; telling a story; past tenses.	Personal characteristics.	Predicting; dealing with unfamiliar words; understanding the writer's style; evaluating the text; reacting to the text.
8 Fun on skis	Telling a story; past tenses.	Skiing; humorous anecdotes.	Predicting; inferring; reacting to the text.
9 Loneliness	Describing feelings and moods.	Relations with people.	Predicting; extracting main ideas; dealing with unfamiliar words; reading for specific information.
10 How would you like to spend the night with him?	Talking about professional abilities; present tense.	Law and order; the police.	Evaluating the text; linking ideas; reading for specific information; dealing with unfamiliar words; reacting to the text.
11 How well do you travel?	Complaining; describing behaviour and personal characteristics.	Holidays; tourism.	Evaluating the text; dealing with unfamiliar words.

Unit	Functions/Structural areas	Vocabulary areas	Reading strategies
12 Homesickness	Telling a story; past tenses; describing feelings.	Feelings.	Extracting main ideas; reading for specific information; understanding the writer's style; reacting to the text.
13 American dreams decoded	Describing habits and behaviour; present simple tense.	Weather; shopping.	Predicting; extracting main ideas; dealing with unfamiliar words; reading for specific information; evaluating the text; inferring; understanding the writer's style; reacting to the text.
14 The aqueduct	Describing constructions; telling a story; past tenses.	Politics and human nature.	Extracting main ideas; evaluating the text; inferring; understanding the writer's style; reacting to the text.
15 Traveler	Describing people and places; describing feelings.	People and relationships.	Predicting; inferring; evaluating the text; extracting main ideas; understanding the writer's style.
16 Accidental discoveries	Describing discoveries and inventions; the passive; past tenses.	Scientific experiments; discoveries.	Predicting; reading for specific information; extracting main ideas; reacting to the text.
17 Love and marriage	Talking about feelings.	Human relations.	Predicting; extracting main ideas; reading for specific information.
18 Hospitality	Describing customs and traditions; telling a story; past tenses.	Behaviour; customs.	Predicting; inferring; evaluating the text; extracting main ideas; reading for specific information.
19 Mazes	Describing how things are built; the passive.		Extracting main ideas; reading for specific information; linking ideas; inferring; dealing with unfamiliar words.
20 Crane diver	Describing feelings; describing a place.	Feelings; a city landscape.	Predicting; extracting main ideas; evaluating the text; inferring; dealing with unfamiliar words; understanding the writer's style.

Thanks

We would like to thank:

Jeanne McCarten, Alison Silver, Lindsay White, Peter Ducker, Amanda Ogden and everybody at Cambridge University Press for making this book possible.

Adrian Doff and the other readers for their extremely helpful comments on the first draft.

The authors and publishers would like to thank the following teachers and their students for piloting *Reading 3*:

Lilias Adam, Institute for Applied Language Studies, University of Edinburgh; Dominic Fisher, Filton Technical College, Bristol; Carol Hunter, ELT Department, Polytechnic of West London and Clare West, English Language Centre, Hove.

Their detailed comments and constructive suggestions made an invaluable contribution to this book.

1 | Lies

1   This unit is about telling lies. Do you always tell the truth? Do you think it's all right to tell lies? If so, in what circumstances?

2   The passage on page 2 comes from a book called *Great Lies* by Jo Donnelly. The opening sentence of the passage is:

> Every day – in every area of our lives – we make and take a thousand lies.

Do you think this is true?

3   Read the passage (on the next page) and find out if the writer approves or disapproves of telling lies.

1

Every day – in every area of our lives – we make and take a thousand lies. Not vicious lies. Not harmful lies. Not lies that count. No, of course not. But great lies. It'll be ready in an hour. Your cheque is in the post. Fresh today. I'll just have one. I was about to call you. Nothing like this has ever happened before. Of course I've never loved anyone else. We pretend, with no effort and less guilt, that we don't lie through our teeth every minute of the day – and everyone else pretends that they don't either. But lying saves time and angst. It makes everybody happier than they would be if they always told or had to listen to the truth. After all, you don't really want to hear that you'll be lucky if you ever see your stereo again. Finding out that you're not going to get paid, at least for a few months, plays havoc with your stress levels. Why should you want to know that the last head of cabbage in the shop – needed urgently for the borscht you're making for the Prime Minister's dinner party – has been sitting under the cash register with the cat for the last two weeks? You're hardly going to make a public announcement that you're about to eat an entire family-size bag of crisps. Not likely. Nor is it likely that you're going to explain to the man about to buy your car that the door always falls off like that. You're certainly not about to tell your fiancé that you loved the man you dated all through university a lot more than you'll ever love him. Think of it like this: life is an incredibly complicated, intricate, fragile, sensitive and dodgy machine – not great, perhaps, but the only one we've got – and lies are the lubricant that keeps the whole thing from blowing in our faces.

Do you agree with the writer?

4 Look at these lies from the passage.

1 It'll be ready in an hour.
2 Your cheque is in the post.
3 Fresh today.
4 I'll just have one.
5 I was about to call you.
6 Nothing like this has ever happened before.
7 Of course I've never loved anyone else.

Read the passage again carefully and match the lies with the truths they conceal. Which lie cannot be matched with a truth? What do you think the truth is?

5 Look at these sentences from the passage. Which ones give justification for telling lies?

1 It'll be ready in an hour.
2 I was about to call you.
3 But lying saves time and angst.
4 It makes everybody happier than they would be if they always told or had to listen to the truth.
5 Life is incredibly complicated … and lies are the lubricant that keeps the whole thing from blowing in our faces.

Can you think of any other good reasons for telling lies?

6 Here are some more examples of lies that people often tell each other. Can you think of a possible context for each sentence and say what truth each lie conceals?

Mothers' lies
You wouldn't like it.
You'll be too tired.
It's not going to hurt you.
There's nothing to be afraid of.

Fathers' lies
I'm busy right now.
It has nothing to do with me. You'll have to ask your mother.
I never said any such thing.

Parents' lies
We're not mad at you, we just want to know what happened.
You can always tell us the truth.
You can talk to us about anything.

7 Can you think of any lies which children tell their parents?

Turn to the *Answer key* for some suggestions.

8 Read the following lies and decide if you have ever told any of them.

Great guest lies
I'm sorry I'm late.
I got lost.
Oh no, it wasn't your directions.
You must give me the recipe.
This is delicious, but I have such a small appetite.
What interesting friends you have.

Great party lies
Everybody will be there.
It won't be the same without you.
It's the best party I've ever been to.
Your friends from work are so entertaining.
I'm sorry I have to go so soon.
I'm fine to drive home.

Telephone lies
I just got in.
I was just going out.
I'll have to ring you back, someone wants to use the phone.
He's out at the moment.
I was here all night. I never heard it ring.
I did ring back but the line was engaged.

Drivers' lies
There's nothing to be nervous about.
It certainly wasn't my fault.
I was only doing thirty.
I never lose my temper behind the wheel.

When was the last time you told a lie? Was it a serious one?

2 | Coincidences

> **coincidence** /kəʊɪnsəˈdəns/, **coincidences**. 1 A **coincidence** is what happens when two or more things occur at the same time by chance in a way that is surprising.

Collins COBUILD dictionary

1 In the passages on page 6 a number of people write about their personal experiences of coincidences. Before you read the passages, look at these headings and think about the kind of coincidence you might read about in each one.

    Small world   Dreams   Intuition

2 Read the passages on the next page and match them with the headings in Exercise 1. The same heading can be used with more than one passage.

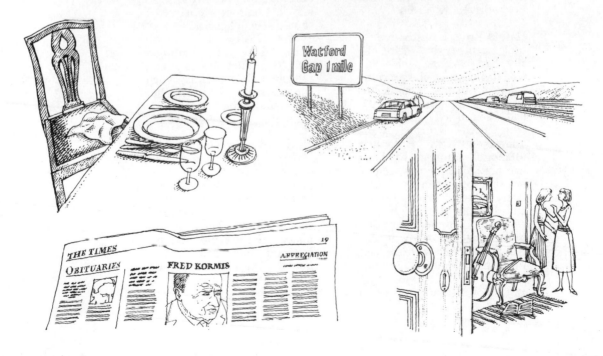

A In November 1981, a Londoner, Andrew Hudson, was being driven to Manchester along the M1 in a white Ford car by Ian Jardin, a civil servant. Nearing the Watford Gap, Jardin began to have trouble accelerating; he pulled on to the hard shoulder, and put through a call for assistance, which duly arrived, and they were able to set out again an hour and a half later.

The following Easter, Hudson found himself being driven along the same stretch of the M1 by Dr Stephen Satterthwaite, of British Steel.

Shortly after they had passed the spot where the trouble had occurred four months earlier, Satterthwaite began to have trouble accelerating, pulled on to the hard shoulder, and rang for assistance. Hudson got out to await the arrival of the AA man.

As he stood by the side of the motorway, he saw a familiar-looking car approaching. It was the white Ford, driven by Jardin.

B Harold Rose, a retired industrial scientist, has occasionally had dreams which his wife dismisses as chance coincidence; but one is harder to explain away. In 1984 they had been briefly acquainted with Fred Kormis, well-known for his Holocaust Memorial sculptures. They had not subsequently seen or heard of him when, two years later, 'I woke one morning, and because I thought my wife would immediately dismiss the subject of my dream, I impressed her with the fact that I had dreamt that morning, just before waking, that Fred Kormis had died. Two days later his obituary appeared in *The Times*.'

When he checked with the director of the art gallery with which the sculptor was connected, he found that Kormis had died on the morning of the dream.

C In 1941, Mrs Ilona Kearey, unable to find work in London, was about to return to the family cottage in the country. On her last day, depressed, she was alone in the flat where she had been staying with friends, playing their piano.

'After a while, I heard the sound of a cello being played solo in the flat directly above me. I listened and became convinced I knew that tone. When I was 11, I had studied the cello for two years, and had made a friend who was 10 at the time. We had gradually drifted apart, and it was about eight years since we had last met. I decided to go up one flight and knock on the door. It was opened by my friend, now 22 and successful. I told her my wish to stay in London; she agreed I should stay in her flat.'

Mrs Kearey stayed with her for three years, finding a war job. They became and remained close friends; when she married, 'I became her son's godmother, and she is godmother to my eldest son.'

D Having dinner with a friend in 1980, Joan Harper recalls, she expected to stay until around 11 o'clock. 'I was just about to begin eating when I had the strongest feeling I should return home immediately. This I did and my husband had just had a massive heart attack. I was able to get medical help and he survived.'

3 Answer the questions about these words or expressions:

Passage A
1 *hard shoulder*: When they had trouble with the car, did they drive (a) in the middle of the road, or (b) to the side of the road?
2 *AA man*: This person is likely to (a) know nothing about cars, or (b) mend the car.

Passage B
3 *dismiss*: Did he think his wife would (a) take him seriously, or (b) not listen to him?
4 *obituary*: This is likely to be (a) a description in a newspaper of the life of someone who has recently died, or (b) a news photo.

Passage C
5 *depressed*: Was she feeling (a) unhappy, or (b) happy?
6 *drifted apart*: (a) Did they intend to stop seeing each other, or (b) was it a slow process of separation?

4 The summaries below are not quite accurate. Rewrite them adding any necessary information or changing information which is wrong.

A Mr Hudson's car broke down twice in four months in the same place and for the same reason. Each time he was in the same car but he had a different driver. The second time he broke down, he saw the man who had been driving the car on the first occasion go past him on the motorway.

B Mr Rose dreamt that a man he had never met, called Fred Kormis, had died. Two days later he read the man's obituary in the newspaper.

C Mrs Keary was a musician. When she heard someone playing the cello in the flat above hers, she went upstairs and introduced herself to the woman who lived there. They made friends immediately and the woman helped Mrs Keary find a job in London.

D Mrs Harper was worried about her husband who was not well. A strong feeling made her decide to go home early and she was able to save her husband's life.

5 Which passage do you find the hardest to explain as a coincidence? Do you think coincidences simply happen by chance, or might there be reasons for them which we don't understand or can't explain?

6 Can you remember any coincidence which happened to you or to someone you know? Write a paragraph describing what happened.

3 | Nightmare journeys

1 Look at these photos. Have you ever travelled in conditions like these?

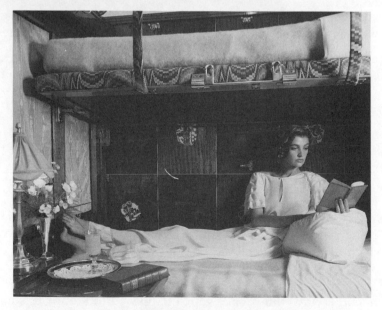

Write down words and expressions which are connected with the situations in the photographs.

2 Read these quotations and decide if each writer feels positive or negative about travel.

1 Whenever I prepare for a journey I prepare as though for death.

Katherine Mansfield, Journal, 1922

2 For my part, I travel not to go anywhere, but to go. I travel for travel's sake. The great affair is to move.

Robert Louis Stephenson, Travels with a Donkey, 1879

3 If God had intended us to fly, he would never have given us railways.

Michael Flanders (attrib.)

4 *What gives value to travel is fear . . . There is no pleasure in travelling, and I look upon it more as an occasion for spiritual testing.*

Albert Camus, Notebooks, 1962

5 I'll take three hours in the dentist's waiting room, with four cavities and an impacted wisdom tooth, in preference to fifteen minutes at any airport waiting for an aeroplane.

Patrick Campbell, Daily Mail, 1947

6 *My heart is warm with the friends I make,*
And better friends I'll not be knowing;
Yet there isn't a train I wouldn't take
No matter where it's going.

Edna St Vincent Millay, 'Travel', Collected Poems, 1956

Which of the quotations do you agree with?

3 The passage on page 11 describes a flight from Hong Kong to London. Read it and find six reasons why the flight was delayed.

4 The writer sometimes exaggerates how he feels about the delay, and sometimes he understates his feelings by leaving out details which he hopes the reader will infer. Answer the questions.

1 *When we discover he has a false passport, we all agree.*
Why do the passengers all agree? Who do they think the man might be?

2 *Those shouting loudest are being given rooms first. I finally get one.*
What is the writer trying to suggest by using the word *finally*?

3 *We are to be allowed a three-minute call each. Isn't that what prisoners get?*
How does the writer feel about his treatment?

4 *A disaster movie camaraderie has seized most of the passengers.*
What does the writer mean by *disaster movie camaraderie*?

5 *In the gloom, the captain's voice echoes over the speaker. He seems much older.*
Why does he *seem older*?

6 *'This is one of the nicest messages you've ever heard. Cabin crew, doors to automatic please.'*
Why is it one of the nicest messages they've ever heard?

7 What does the writer mean by the last two sentences? *Is it churlish ... I'm feeling pretty churlish.*

Can you find any other occasions when the writer exaggerates or understates his feelings?

5 Do you think the way the writer conveys his feelings is effective? Do you think he can say who is to blame? Is there a quotation in Exercise 2 which reflects his attitude towards his nightmare journey?

6 Look through the passage again and add to the list you made in Exercise 1 any new words which are connected with flying or travelling.

7 Have you ever had a journey which has turned into a nightmare? Whose fault was it: the passengers, the weather, the means of transport or some other reason? Write a paragraph describing what happened and how you felt. You may like to use 'Hong Kong high jinx' as a model.

Hong Kong high jinx

James Long relives a plane trip that turned into a very long haul indeed

Kai Tak Airport, Hong Kong. Friday, 10.45pm: The 747 is packed and it's minutes after the scheduled departure time. The captain tells us a passenger has been arrested at emigration, and they need to find his bags in the hold before we can fly. When we discover he has a false passport, we all agree.

11.15pm: 'I'm afraid this is turning into a bit of a saga, Ladies and Gentlemen. We haven't been able to find the bags so we have to offload all the containers and search them. That means that the crew will exceed its maximum hours and we'll have to organise a stop-over somewhere in Europe to take on a replacement crew.'

11.55pm: 'You'll be pleased to hear we have now found and removed the suspect bags. Unfortunately, we haven't yet been able to organise another crew.'

Midnight: As the clock strikes, Kai Tak airport turns into a pumpkin and shuts down for the night. The crew go off to bed, the first- and second-class passengers are taken to the nearby Airport Hotel and the economy-class begin a mystery tour.

Saturday, 2.30am: In the hotel foyer the scene is dreadful. We are being asked to share rooms with total strangers. I am travelling with a colleague. 'Double room', they insist. I point out she is of a different sex and we've only known each other a week.

3.30am: Those shouting loudest are being given rooms

first. I finally get one. Now everyone wants to call the UK to rearrange disrupted schedules. Our hosts regard this as unreasonable and far too expensive. We can't even call at our own cost because they've locked the phones. At last we reach a compromise. We are to be allowed a three-minute call each. Isn't that what prisoners get?

11.30am: We check out. The hotel tries to argue that my phone call was 31 seconds longer than agreed.

2.55pm: With five minutes to take-off, the captain comes on the intercom. You can tell from the way he clears his throat that he is not relishing this. 'I'm very sorry indeed to tell you that we have a minor avionics problem. We are doing our very best to fix it and I'll keep you informed.' A disaster movie camaraderie has seized most of the passengers. My colleague claims they're all working out whom they'd sleep with first. I'm trying to decide which one I'd eat.

5.55pm: By now we're all familiar with the Boeing 747-400's fuel system. The tail tank isn't talking to the wing tanks, so the plane would probably belly-flop on take-off unless they can fix it. They pump fuel out, move the freight around to balance it, and eventually solve the problem by phoning Boeing in Seattle.

6.00pm: We're ready to go . . . to Copenhagen. Yes,

the crew's allowable hours of work are once again running out.

11.45pm, Copenhagen: Our inflight magazine says they are trying to win the hearts and minds of travellers because an 'airline interacts with its consumers over long periods of time'.

We're on the ground at Copenhagen, over 32 hours into our 14-hour flight, saying goodbye to a crew which has been interacting with its consumers for much longer than the training course ever anticipated, with unrelenting cheerfulness. The new crew arrive fully briefed: they're expecting a rebellion. Our new captain says we are taking off in five minutes. Almost immediately, the lights go out. Dim emergency lighting comes on. In the gloom, the captain's voice echoes over the speaker. He seems much older. 'Ladies and Gentlemen, we do seem to have a small problem with the electrical system.'

Midnight: 'Ladies and Gentlemen. This is one of the nicest messages you've ever heard. Cabin crew, doors to automatic please.'

Sunday, 1.30am: We land at Heathrow 37 hours after checking in at Hong Kong. I bully the airline into providing a car to drive me home. Is it churlish of me to mention that the driver claims never to have driven in the dark and grinds to a halt every time a car comes the other way? By the time I get to bed at 4.30am I'm feeling pretty churlish.

4 | The cow that ate the piper

In this unit there is a short folktale from Ireland, translated from the Irish language by Sean O'Sullivan. As a folktale, it belongs to an oral tradition of storytelling, and was probably only written down when it was translated. There are a few words and constructions which belong to the Irish English dialect, but which you should be able to understand from their context. For example, a *spalpeen* is an old word for a workman.

1 Before you read *The Cow that ate the Piper*, do you know what the features of folktales told by storytellers might be? Are they very different to the features of the modern novel?

2 Every story has at least one 'pivotal point' around which the plot turns. Without a pivotal point, a story would simply be a description of an event or an emotion. Read *The Cow that ate the Piper* on page 13, and decide what you think its pivotal point is.

The Cow that ate the Piper

There were three spalpeens coming home to Kerry from Limerick one time after working there. On their way, they met a piper on the road.

'I'll go along with ye,' said the piper.

'All right,' they said.

The night was very cold, freezing hard, and they were going to perish. They saw a dead man on the road with a new pair of shoes on his feet.

'By heavens!' said the piper. 'I haven't a stitch of shoes on me. Give me that spade to see (*sic*) can I cut off his legs.'

'Twas the only way he could take off the shoes. They were held on by the frost. So he took hold of the spade and cut off the two feet at the ankles. He took them along with him. They got lodgings at a house where three cows were tied in the kitchen.

'Keep away from that grey cow,' said the servant girl, 'or she'll eat your coats. Keep out from her.'

They all went to sleep. The three spalpeens and the piper stretched down near the fire. The piper heated the shoes and the dead man's feet at the fire and got the shoes off. When the servant girl got up, she looked at the door. It was bolted, and the three spalpeens were asleep near the fire.

'My God!' she cried. 'There were four of ye last night, and now there are only three. Where did the other man go?'

'We don't know,' they said. 'How would we know where he went?'

She went to the grey cow's head and found the two feet.

'Oh my!' she cried. 'He was eaten by her.'

She called the man of the house.

'The grey cow has eaten one of the men,' said she.

'What's that you're saying?' said the farmer.

'I'm telling the truth,' said she. 'There's only his feet left. The rest of him is eaten.'

The farmer got up. 'There were four of ye there last night, men,' said he.

'There were,' said one of the spalpeens, 'and our comrade has been eaten by the cow.'

'Don't cause any trouble about it,' said the farmer. 'Here's five pounds for ye. Eat your breakfast and be off. Don't say a word.'

They left when they had the breakfast eaten. And they met the piper some distance from the house, and he dancing on the road. Such a thing could happen!

3 Did you enjoy the folktale? Is there anything which surprises or shocks you? If so, can you explain why?

4 Read the *The Cow that ate the Piper* again and underline the sentences which describe the storyline. What is the function of the extra information?

5 Look at these sentences:

1 One very cold night, three workmen and a piper found a dead man with new shoes lying on the road.
2 The piper was very poor.

Sentence 1 summarises the facts of the folktale, and sentence 2 interprets them.

Now read the following sentences. Which ones summarise the facts, and which ones interpret them?

3 The piper did not have any shoes, so he wanted the ones the dead man was wearing.
4 New shoes were valuable; a dead man was not.
5 They stayed overnight in a farm; in the kitchen there were three cows.
6 The warm fire allowed the piper to get the shoes off the dead man's feet.
7 The piper deliberately put the feet near the grey cow to make it seem as if the cow had eaten him.
8 The piper left early next morning.
9 One of the spalpeens bolted the door behind him.
10 The servant came in and saw there were only three men there.
11 By the grey cow were a pair of feet, and she thought the cow had eaten the missing man.
12 The farmer paid the three men to keep quiet about the dead man.
13 The farmer was worried that he would be in trouble about the dead man.
14 The piper was waiting for them.
15 It was all a trick to get some money from the farmer.

6 Look at the sentences in Exercise 5 which interpret the facts. Do you agree with the interpretation? Can you think of any other interpretation?

7 Look at the sentences in Exercise 5 which summarise the facts. Use them to write a summary of the folktale. Add any details which reveal your own interpretation of the story.

14

8   Look for details in *The Cow that ate the Piper* which tell you something
     about life and society in Ireland at the time. Are there any details which
     are different from life and society in your country? When do you think the
     folktale was set?

9   Think about folktales in your culture. Do you know if they were written
     or spoken? Do you know who the authors were or where the folktales
     came from?

     Write a paragraph telling a folktale from your culture. You may like to use
     The Cow that ate the Piper as a model.

5 | He was a good lion

1 The animals in the photos are wild animals. Do you think they are likely to make good pets? How would you feel if you were in a room with one of these animals? Would you like to have one of these animals as a pet?

2 The passages which follow are taken from *He was a Good Lion* by Beryl Markham, an English writer who lived in Kenya. Read the first part of the account and decide which of these statements about the lion is true.

1 Paddy was a tame lion that lived on the farm.
2 Paddy had been captured and kept in a cage when he was very young.
3 Paddy was free to go wherever he wanted.
4 Paddy could not return to the wild because the other lions would reject him.
5 No one believed Paddy was dangerous.

> The Elkington lion was famous within a radius of twelve miles from the farm, because, if you happened to be anywhere inside that circle, you would hear him roar when he was hungry, when he was sad, or when he just felt like roaring.
>
> Two or three of the settlers in East Africa at that time had caught lion cubs and raised them in cages. But Paddy, the Elkington lion, had never seen a cage.
>
> He had grown full size, tawny, black-maned and muscular, without a worry or a care. He lived on fresh meat, not of his own killing. He spent his waking hours (which coincided with everyone else's sleeping hours) wandering through Elkington's fields and pastures like an emperor in the gardens of his court.
>
> There were no physical barriers to his freedom, but the lions of the plains do not accept into their respected fraternity an individual bearing in his coat the smell of men. So Paddy ate, slept, and roared, and perhaps he sometimes dreamed, but he never left Elkington's. He was a tame lion, Paddy was. He was deaf to the call of the wild.
>
> 'I'm always careful of that lion,' I told my father, 'but he's really harmless. I've seen Mrs Elkington stroke him.'
>
> 'Which proves nothing,' said my father. 'A domesticated lion is only an unnatural lion – and whatever is unnatural is untrustworthy.'

3 Read the last two sentences again. What do you expect to happen?

Now read the next part of the account and see if you were right.

I was within twenty yards of the Elkington lion before I saw him. I stopped running and he lifted his head with magnificent ease and stared at me out of yellow eyes.

I stood there staring back, scuffling my bare toes in the dust, pursing my lips to make a noiseless whistle – a very small girl who knew about lions. Paddy raised himself then, emitting a little sigh, and began to contemplate me with a kind of quiet premeditation.

I cannot say that there was any menace in his eyes, because there wasn't. He did sniff the air though, and he did not lie down again.

I remembered the rules that one remembers. I did not run. I walked very slowly, and I began to sing a defiant song.

'Kali coma Simba sisi,' I sang. I went in a straight line past Paddy when I sang it, seeing his eyes shine in the thick grass, watching his tail beat time to the metre of my ditty.

'Twendi, twendi – ku pigana – piga aduoi – piga sana! – Let us go, let us go – to fight – beat down the enemy! Beat hard, beat hard!'

What lion would be unimpressed with the marching song of the King's African Rifles?

Singing it still, I took up my trot toward the rim of the low hill which might, if I were lucky, have Cape gooseberry bushes on its slopes.

The country was grey-green and dry, and the sun lay on it closely, making the ground hot under my bare feet. There was no sound and no wind. Even Paddy made no sound, coming swiftly behind me.

What I remember most clearly of the moment that followed are three things – a scream that was barely a whisper, a blow that struck me to the ground, and, as I buried my face in my arms and felt Paddy's teeth close on the flesh of my leg, a fantastically bobbing turban, that was Bishon Singh's turban, appear over the edge of the hill.

I remained conscious, but I closed my eyes and tried not to be. It was not so much the pain as it was the sound. The sound of Paddy's roaring in my ears will never be duplicated. It was an immense roar that encompassed the world and dissolved me in it.

I shut my eyes very tight and lay still under the weight of Paddy's paws.

4 Choose four or five words which are difficult to understand. Can you guess their meaning from the context?

Here are the definitions, in the context of the passage, of some of the difficult words. Do any of these definitions match the words you have chosen?

making a scratching and scraping sound with something
giving or sending out
a deep breath that others can hear
a well-planned intention
draw in air loudly through the nose
openly unafraid
a simple song
a slow run
very quickly
a headcovering worn by Muslims, Sikhs and Hindus
aware of what is happening
surrounded

5 Answer the questions:

1 How old was the writer when she was attacked by the lion?
2 She writes 'I remembered the rules that one remembers.' What rules is she referring to?
3 Was she frightened of the lion as she walked past it?
4 Who saw the lion attack her?
5 Did the lion give warning that it was going to attack?

6 What do you think happened next?

Now read the following summary of what happened.

Bishon Singh, who worked on the Elkington farm, had seen the lion following the girl and he had shouted for help. Just as the lion attacked her, Mr Elkington appeared and rushed at it with a long stick. The lion deserted the girl and ran towards Mr Elkington who dropped his stick and climbed a nearby tree. Meanwhile, Bishon Singh picked up the girl and carried her to the house.

7 Read the end of the account. How does the writer feel about the lion today? 🗝

> That night he killed a horse, and the next night he killed a yearling bullock, and after that a cow fresh for milking.
>
> In the end he was caught and finally caged, but brought to no rendezvous with the firing squad at sunrise. He remained for years in his cage, which, had he managed to live in freedom with his inhibitions, he might never have seen at all.
>
> It seems characteristic of the mind of man that the repression of what is natural to humans must be abhorred, but that what is natural to an infinitely more natural animal must be confined within the bounds of reason peculiar only to men.
>
> Paddy lived, people stared at him and he stared back, and he went on until he was an old, old lion. Jim Elkington died, and Mrs Elkington, who really loved Paddy, was forced, because of circumstances beyond her control or Paddy's, to have him shot by Boy Long, the manager of Lord Delamere's estate.
>
> This choice of executioners was, in itself, a tribute to Paddy, for no one loved animals more or understood them better, or could shoot more cleanly than Boy Long.
>
> But the result was the same to Paddy. He had lived and died in ways not of his choosing. He was a good lion. He had done what he could about being a tame lion. Who thinks it just to be judged by a single error?
>
> I still have the scars of his teeth and claws, but they are very small now and almost forgotten, and I cannot begrudge him his moment.

8 Which of these statements do you think the writer would agree with? 🗝

1 Wild animals that live with people cannot be expected to keep their natural instincts under control all the time.
2 Wild animals that live with people are unnatural because they behave like humans.
3 Wild animals do not choose to be brought up in captivity and can only adapt as best they can to an unnatural way of life.
4 Wild animals which live in captivity are very lucky because they often live for much longer than they would in the wild.

Which statements do you agree with?

9 Do you think it is a good thing to keep a wild animal in captivity? What are the advantages of keeping animals in captivity, for example, in zoos? Have you ever tried to tame a wild animal?

6 | Bargains

1 The title of this unit is *Bargains*. Here are some possible definitions of the word. Which ones do you agree with?

1 a goodwill gesture made by shopkeepers to their customers
2 a selling technique
3 something sold at an unusually low price
4 an opportunity not to be missed
5 a trick to make you buy something that you do not really want

The passage on page 22 is from *How to be poor* by George Mikes, a Hungarian writer who lived in Britain. Read the first two paragraphs of the passage and decide which definition he would agree with.

1 Let us take the orthodox definition of the word *bargain*. It is something offered at a low and advantageous price. It is an opportunity to buy something at a lower price than it is really worth. A more recent definition is: a bargain is a dirty trick to extort money from the pockets of silly and innocent people.

2 I have never attended a large company's board meeting in my life, but I feel certain that the discussion often takes the following lines. The cost of producing a new – for example – toothpaste would make 80p the decent price for it, so we will market it at £1.20. It is not a bad toothpaste (not specially good either, but not bad), and as people like to try new things it will sell well to start with; but the attraction of novelty soon fades, so sales will fall. When that starts to happen we will reduce the price to £1.15. And we will turn it into a bargain by printing 5p OFF all over it, whereupon people will rush to buy it even though it still costs about forty-three per cent more than its fair price.

Sometimes it is not 5p OFF but 1p OFF. What breathtaking impertinence to advertise 1p OFF your soap or washing powder or dog food or whatever. Even the poorest old-age pensioner ought to regard this as an insult, but he doesn't. A bargain must not be missed. To be offered a 'gift' of one penny is like being invited to dinner and offered one single pea (tastily cooked), and nothing else. Even if it represented a real reduction it would be an insult.

3 Still, people say, one has to have washing powder (or whatever) and one might as well buy it a penny cheaper. When I was a boy in Hungary a man was accused of murdering someone for the sake of one pengo, the equivalent of a shilling, and pleaded guilty. The judge was outraged: 'To kill a man for a shilling! . . . What can you say in your defence?' The murderer replied: 'A shilling here . . . a shilling there . . .' And that's what today's shopper says, too: 'A penny here . . . a penny there . . .'

The real danger starts when utterly unnecessary things become 'bargains'. There is a huge number of people who just cannot resist bargains

2 Read the rest of the passage and decide which paragraphs are about:

a) how a new product is sold
b) buying in large quantities
c) defining what a 'bargain' is
d) how the writer feels about people who waste money on bargains
e) an unusual way of 'making' money
f) things people buy just because they are bargains
g) how people react to small price reductions

and sales. Provided they think they are getting a bargain they will buy clothes they will never wear, furniture they have no space for. Old ladies will buy roller-skates and non-smokers will buy pipe-cleaners. And I once heard of a man who bought an electric circular saw as a bargain and cut off two of his fingers the next day. But he had no regrets: the saw had been truly cheap.

Quite a few people actually believe that they make money on such bargains. A lady I know, otherwise a charming and seemingly sane girl, sometimes tells me stories such as this: 'I've had a lucky day today. I bought a dress for £120, reduced from £400; I bought a suitcase for £40, reduced from £120 and I bought a beautiful Persian carpet for £600, reduced from £900.' Perhaps she may add vaguely that she has been a trifle extravagant, but it will never occur to her that she has actually wasted £760. She feels as though she has *made* £660. She also feels, I am sure, that if she had more time for shopping, she could make a living out of it.

Some people buy in bulk because it is cheaper. At certain moments New Zealand lamb chops may be 3p cheaper if you buy half a ton of them, so people rush to buy a freezer just to find out later that it is too small to hold half a ton of New Zealand lamb. I once knew a couple who could not resist buying sugar in bulk. They thought it a tremendous bargain, not to be missed, so they bought enough sugar for their lifetime and the lifetime of their children and grandchildren. When the sugar arrived they didn't know where to store it – until they realised that their loo was a very spacious one. So that was where they piled up their sugar. Not only did their guests feel rather strange whenever they were offered sugar to put into their coffee, but the loo became extremely sticky.

To offer bargains is a commercial trick to make the poor poorer. When greedy fools fall for this trick, it serves them right. All the same, if bargains were prohibited by law our standard of living would immediately rise by 7.39 per cent.

3 Answer the questions about these words and expressions: 🗝

1 *the attraction of novelty soon fades*: Are (a) more, or (b) fewer people likely to buy the product?
2 *breathtaking impertinence*: Is this (a) unbelievable rudeness, (b) a waste of time, or (c) a clever sales technique?
3 *in bulk*: Does buying in bulk mean (a) buying in large quantities, (b) buying as much as you can, or (c) buying too much?
4 *it serves them right*: Is the writer (a) sympathetic, or (b) unsympathetic towards people who are tricked into buying bargains?

4   Look at the following general statements. Can you find examples in the passage which illustrate these statements?

1   Bargains are often a way of making expensive products look cheap.
2   Very small price reductions are an insult to the customer.
3   People often buy things they don't want because they are bargains.
4   Some people seem to believe that they make money when they buy a bargain.
5   Buying in bulk is often thought to be a cheap way of buying.
6   People like to try new products.
7   People react in the same way to small price reductions as they do to big ones.

5   The writer creates a humorous effect by the use of exaggeration. For example: 'Old ladies will buy roller-skates ...'

Can you find any more examples of amusing exaggeration in the passage?

6   Do you look around the shops for bargains? Have you ever bought anything that you didn't need just because you thought it was a bargain? What was the best bargain you have found?

7   Bargaining also means negotiating to bring the price down. In what circumstances can you bargain in your country?

7 | A lamp in a window

1 The short story in this unit is by the American writer Truman Capote. Some of the vocabulary and spelling is American English. In the first part of *A Lamp in the Window*, the writer finds himself a passenger in the car of a drunken driver. Have you ever been in this situation? What did you do? What would you do?

2 Read the first part of the story and find out what the writer did.

Once I was invited to a wedding; the bride suggested I drive up from New York with a pair of other guests, a Mr and Mrs Roberts, whom I had never met before. It was a cold April day, and on the ride to Connecticut the Robertses, a couple in their early forties, seemed agreeable enough – no one you would want to spend a long weekend with, but not bad.

However at the wedding reception a great deal of liquor was consumed, I should say a third of it by my chauffeurs. They were the last to leave the party – at approximately 11pm – and I was most wary of accompanying them; I knew they were drunk, but I didn't realize *how* drunk. We had driven about twenty miles, the car weaving considerably, and Mr and Mrs Roberts insulting each other in the most extraordinary language, when Mr Roberts very understandably made a wrong turn and got lost on a dark country road. I kept asking them, finally begging them, to stop the car and let me out, but they were so involved in their invectives that they ignored me. Eventually the car stopped of its own accord (temporarily) when it swiped against the side of a tree. I used the opportunity to jump out the car's back door and run into the woods. Presently the cursed vehicle drove off, leaving me alone in the icy dark. I'm sure my hosts never missed me; Lord knows I didn't miss them.

3 Choose four or five words which are difficult to understand. Can you guess their meaning from the context?

Here are the definitions, in the context of the passage, of some of the difficult words. Do any of these definitions match the words you have chosen?

drunk   cautious   driving from side to side
insults   crashed

4 Can you guess what the writer did next? Think about these questions:

Where was he?
What time was it?
What was the weather like?
Where did he want to go?

5 Read on and see if your guesses were right.

But it wasn't a joy to be stranded out there on a windy cold night.

I started walking, hoping I'd reach a highway. I walked for half an hour without sighting a habitation. Then, just off the road, I saw a small frame cottage with a porch and a window lighted by a lamp. I tiptoed onto the porch and looked in the window; an elderly woman with soft white hair and a round pleasant face was sitting by a fireside reading a book. There was a cat curled in her lap, and several others sleeping at her feet.

I knocked at the door, and when she opened it I said, with chattering teeth: 'I'm sorry to disturb you, but I've had a sort of accident; I wonder if I could use your phone to call a taxi.'

'Oh, dear,' she said, smiling. 'I'm afraid I don't have a phone. Too poor. But please, come in.' And as I stepped through the door into a cozy room, she said: 'My goodness, boy. You're freezing. Can I make coffee? A cup of tea? I have a little whiskey my husband left – he died six years ago.'

I said a little whiskey would be very welcome.

While she fetched it I warmed my hands at the fire and glanced around the room. It was a cheerful place occupied by six or seven cats of varying colors. I looked at the title of the book Mrs Kelly – for that was her name, as I later learned – had been reading: it was *Emma* by Jane Austen, a favorite writer of mine.

6 The writer uses a number of words and expressions to convey the warm and friendly atmosphere of the house and its occupant. For example: '... an elderly woman with *soft* white hair ...'

Can you find some more examples in the passage?

7 Read the next part of the story. Decide if there is anything which adds to or changes your impression of the old lady. Is there anything which you think may be important for the rest of the story?

When Mrs Kelly returned with a glass of ice and a dusty quarter-bottle of bourbon, she said: 'Sit down, sit down. It's not often I have company. Of course, I have my cats. Anyway, you'll spend the night? I have a nice little guest room that's been waiting such a long time for a guest. In the morning you can walk to the highway and catch a ride into town, where you'll find a garage to fix your car. It's about five miles away.'

I wondered aloud how she could live so isolatedly, without transportation or a telephone; she told me her good friend, the mailman, took care of all her shopping needs. 'Albert. He's really so dear and faithful. But he's due to retire next year. After that I don't know what I'll do. But something will turn up. Perhaps a kindly new mailman. Tell me, just what sort of accident did you have?'

When I explained the truth of the matter, she responded indignantly: 'You did exactly the right thing. I wouldn't set foot in a car with a man who had sniffed a glass of sherry. That's how I lost my husband. Married forty years, forty happy years, and I lost him because a drunken driver ran him down. If it wasn't for my cats . . .' She stroked an orange tabby purring in her lap.

8 The following words or expressions are more frequent in American English. What are their equivalents in British English?

bourbon   highway   catch a ride   fix your car
transportation   mailman

27

9 Read the next part of the story and see if your impressions in Exercise 7 are confirmed.

>   We talked by the fire until my eyes grew heavy. We talked about Jane Austen ('Ah, Jane. My tragedy is that I've read all her books so often I have them memorized'), and other admired authors: Thoreau, Willa Cather, Dickens, Lewis Carroll, Agatha Christie, Raymond Chandler, Hawthorne, Chekhov, De Maupassant – she was a woman with a good and varied mind; intelligence illuminated her hazel eyes like the small lamp shining on the table beside her. We talked about the hard Connecticut winters, politicians, far places ('I've never been abroad, but if ever I'd had the chance, the place I would have gone is Africa. Sometimes I've dreamed of it, the green hills, the heat, the beautiful giraffes, the elephants walking about'), religion ('Of course, I was raised a Catholic, but now, I'm almost sorry to say, I have an open mind. Too much reading, perhaps'), gardening ('I grow and can all my own vegetables; a necessity'). At last: 'Forgive my babbling on. You have no idea how much pleasure it gives me. But it's way past your bedtime. I know it is mine.'
>
>   She escorted me upstairs, and after I was comfortably arranged in a double bed under a blissful load of scrapquilts, she returned to wish me good night, sweet dreams. I lay awake thinking about it. What an exceptional experience – to be an old woman living alone here in the wilderness and have a stranger knock on your door in the middle of the night and not only open it but warmly welcome him inside and offer him shelter. If our situations had been reversed, I doubt that I would have had the courage, to say nothing of the generosity.

10 Decide whose opinions are given in brackets, the writer's or the old lady's. What do they tell us about the person?

11 Read the next part of the story. Is there anything which you find strange? Are your impressions in Exercise 7 confirmed?

> The next morning she gave me breakfast in her kitchen. Coffee and hot oatmeal with sugar and tinned cream, but I was hungry and it tasted great. The kitchen was shabbier than the rest of the house; the stove, a rattling refrigerator, everything seemed on the edge of expiring. All except one large, somewhat modern object, a deep-freeze that fitted into a corner of the room.
>
> She was chatting on: 'I love birds. I feel so guilty about not tossing them crumbs during the winter. But I can't have them gathering around the house. Because of the cats. Do you care for cats?'
>
> 'Yes, I once had a Siamese called Toma. She lived to be twelve, and we traveled everywhere together. All over the world. And when she died I never had the heart to get another.'
>
> 'Then maybe you will understand this,' she said, . . .

12 Can you guess how the story ends?

Now turn to page 79 of the *Answer key* and check.

13 How do you feel about the old lady? Do you agree with the writer? Why do you think Truman Capote called this story *A Lamp in a Window*? What do you think he was referring to?

14 How would you react if a stranger knocked on your door late at night?

8 | Fun on skis

1   Have you ever been skiing? If so, did you enjoy it? If not, would you like
    to go? Why? Is it possible to ski in your country?

2   The stories on page 31 were chosen by judges from more than 200 entries
    in the *Observer* competition in which readers were asked to tell a story
    about their 'Funniest moment on skis'. The first prize was a two-week
    skiing holiday in Colorado, USA.

    Decide which of the following words you would expect to see in the
    stories.

    snow   wedding   slope   ice   insult   muscle   panic
    chair lift   refrigerator   slide   bargain   nightmare
    plunge   boot

    You can use a dictionary if necessary.

3   Read the stories on page 31, and decide which ones are shown in the
    pictures.

1 Our first skiing holiday coincided with a shortage of snow and closed nursery slopes. We bravely went through the early exercises on small ice slopes until our muscles cried out.

Next morning we went partway up the main slope. I was at the front and after a demonstration of the 'snow plough' was told to try it out. I did, with my knees carefully together. Unfortunately, the toes of the skis were apart. In the icy conditions, I picked up speed. Panicking, arms flailing, I scattered two other groups of learners before crossing the café balustrade and demolishing chairs and tables.

Pale as a ghost and feeling close to death but with no real injuries, I was relieved to see my wife running up. She looked down, saw I was alive, and said: 'You've found something else you're not very good at.'

2 I was sitting in the centre of a three-man chair; actually I was half on because my desperate attempts to get my bottom into the seat and the bar down failed and, 50 feet from the starting point, I plunged towards deep snow.

But I didn't reach the ground because my boot caught up with the skiers sharing the seat. They were pulled partially off the chair and left half on, supporting my weight while I was suspended upside down.

This happened quickly but we'd gone further up before the operator stopped the lift. This sudden jerk dislodged my left boot, sending me and one of my fellow passengers hurtling to the ground.

I landed on my face, fortunately on soft snow. I turned to see my victim, who landed on his skis, facing uphill, and who slid 30 yards backwards, demolishing a ski class before finally coming to rest.

3 It was the first time I had been on a chair lift. We queued on an icy patch and I lost my hold on the restraining post. Suddenly out of control, I slid forwards between the two skiers who were waiting for the two-man chair to come round the corner behind them. I landed on one seat and one of the others landed on the other. This left the third, an Austrian whose place I had unintentionally taken, thrown roughly across the central bar. The three of us lurched forward about 20 feet until the lift was stopped and the Austrian got down. Feeling more and more ridiculous, I realised that my troubles were not over. In the fracas I had lost one ski and at the summit I would have to ski off the chair lift, down a steep slope completely out of control on one ski. I fell head first into the snow. I heard something falling down beside me. It was my lost ski which the Austrian gentleman sportingly returned to me.

4 My funniest moment on skis happened in Whitefish, Montana. My husband and I were on the ski lift, a new experience to him. Not realising the lift didn't stop, he hesitated before attempting to get off, mistiming completely. He stumbled and hung on to the edge of the chair with his hands. He made history in Whitefish that day. The attendant stared in amazement saying: 'Man oh man. Man oh man. Where'd you say you folks were from?'

By now, a crowd of several dozen people were watching, open mouthed, as my poor, silly husband went around the wheel of the lift, 100 feet in the air, hanging by his fingernails, skis intact, face an unbelievable picture of horror. I laughed – couldn't help it, he looked so ridiculous.

The lift stopped at the station, husband 'alighted' gracefully to the applause of the unexpectedly entertained crowd.

4 Which of the words in Exercise 2 appeared in the stories?

5 The following general statements about skiing are true. Find sentences in the stories to support them.

   a) The correct position for the snow plough is with knees together and toes of the skis touching.
   b) Your skis are more difficult to control when it's icy.
   c) To get on a chair lift you stand in position; when it arrives from behind, you sit down and bring down a safety bar.
   d) At the top, the chair lift doesn't stop to let you get off. You ski down a slope before your chair goes round the wheel.

6 In each story, the 'Funniest moment' was caused by someone making a single mistake. What were the mistakes?

7 Which story would you give the first prize to?

   Turn to page 80 of the *Answer key* and find out which one the judges chose.

8 The writers thought the stories were *funny*. Do you find them funny? Here are some words which can have a similar meaning to *funny*.

   odd   eccentric   amusing   witty   unusual   ridiculous
   absurd

   Which words are closest to the writers' understanding of *funny*? Can you think of more suitable adjectives to describe the stories?

9 Has anything 'funny' ever happened to you or someone you know when you were doing a sport? Write a paragraph telling the story.

9 | Loneliness

Loneliness is more than aloneness. It is minding being alone.

1   Do you like spending time alone? Why? What sort of things do you enjoy doing when you are alone? Have you ever suffered from loneliness? How did you cope with it?

2   Decide which of these groups of people are most likely to suffer from loneliness.

children	teenagers	young mothers	business people
widows/widowers	pensioners	students	divorced people
single parents	foreigners	unemployed people	celebrities

What do you think are the main causes of loneliness for these people?

3

In the passages which follow four people talk about their personal experiences of loneliness. Read the passages and decide which groups in Exercise 2 they belong to.

1

'I used to be a teacher, and when I left work to have Emma I hardly knew my neighbours' names,' she said. 'Being at home with your first baby is a great shock to the system. For six months all my time was taken up by Emma, but she did cry a lot and by the end of the day I could have screamed myself. There was just no one I could phone to talk it over or ask round for coffee. My husband was sympathetic but he was at work, and my mother lives miles away.

'Luckily I'm not the depressive kind, but I did feel terribly isolated. I could go for days without talking to anyone, and then when my husband came home I'd take it out on him when he was tired. I can absolutely understand how the loneliness becomes too much for some women.

'I was told about the National Housewives' Register, which has been my life saver. We have regular meetings, but you don't have to go every time, and it's enormously stimulating not to talk about children. I feel it would have been better if I had planned full-time motherhood in advance, in the same way that people plan their retirement, because it can be just as lonely.'

2

'Before I took up CB[1] I didn't know what to do with myself in the evenings,' she said. 'I had my own TV and record player in my room, and after I had done my homework I'd just stay up there until it was time to go to bed. I got the feeling I was the only person my age in the whole area. I think teenagers are bound to be lonely unless they're involved in a sport or a hobby.

'Most of my school friends don't live near me, and I got so bored and miserable. Even if you do get to go to a disco they aren't really places to meet people if you're shy. I could never think of anything to say. And I really did think I was the only one, until I met a lot of other local 'breakers'[2]. There are ten in my road, at least. At first I was a bit shy about talking to someone I'd never met, but I soon got to know people.

'Going on-channel changes your personality. You do gain confidence by chatting to people. There's nothing to do around here at all and if it wasn't for CB, I'd still be lonely.'

---

1 Citizens' Band radio: two-way radios that people use for talking to other radio owners.
2 People who use CB radios as a hobby.

3

'Loneliness was a new experience for me. At home I had always had plenty of friends,' he said. 'Unfortunately, I arrived at the end of the first term when people had already begun making friends and forming into little groups. I felt very much the outsider. I tried going down to the students' bar but no one bothered to say hello. I would just have to buy myself a drink, drink it, and go back to my room. I did consider giving the course up when the loneliness got too bad, but I knew people at home would be disappointed in me if I did.

'It is harder to make friends when you come from a totally different background. There was a lot about English people I found difficult to understand. They are not very expressive, for one thing. Even when friends meet they will just say "Hi" very casually, whereas at home people will stop, shake hands, give you a hug and ask you how you are. In time, I realised that English people do care, but they have this unwritten rule not to encroach on someone else's space. There is some racism, too.

'There are other cultural differences. I didn't understand the English sense of humour. There seemed to be such a lot of teasing and friendly insults I just wasn't used to.

'I began to feel that there must be something wrong with me. Eventually I went to the Student Advisory Service and also became involved in college politics, so now I feel much more at home. I made a real effort to get to know this year's new students from overseas.

'Loneliness is almost inevitable when you are a stranger in a strange country. Now I have got used to the coolness of English people I know that it doesn't mean they don't care. All the time I was lonely I probably had more friends than I realised.'

4

'I'm sure a lot of people in the media are terribly lonely if they will only admit it,' he said. 'That's why you see them in pubs and wine bars, because they have nowhere else to go. They turn to drink to deaden the effect. Being famous is like being extremely beautiful, in that it makes you seem unapproachable.

'It can be very difficult for someone like me to go into a pub, for instance. People stare, and come over and ask for an autograph, which is very nice and flattering, but the assumption is always: "What on earth is he doing here?" Initially it is very easy to meet people, but it is always very superficial, and they are always the same kind of people.

'I have suffered very badly from loneliness in the past. Like many broadcasters, I am quite shy, but I was also very ambitious, and that didn't leave me much time for friendship.

'Eventually you can begin to enjoy loneliness and stop feeling sorry for yourself. I have a great job which compensates for a lot. I have one really good friend I've known for years, and I feel you can't have everything!'

4

These are the first paragraphs of the passages. Match them with the passages.

a) George Okide is a post-graduate from Nigeria who came to Britain to study for a PhD at Chelsea College.

b) Sheila Rush has experienced a particularly modern style of loneliness – the loneliness of the working wife transformed into a suburban mother. Sheila, her husband and two small children have now moved house four times in six years because of her husband's job.

c) Radio DJ Tony Blackburn agrees that loneliness is no respecter of persons, and that being in the public eye can make you feel extremely isolated.

d) Lynn Curtis is 16 and lives in a suburb where there are few facilities for young people her age. Those that do exist are only accessible by expensive public transport. Lynn was extremely lonely until six months ago when she bought a Citizens' Band radio. Now she is on-channel most nights of the week and her life has been transformed.

Which of these experiences of loneliness do you find the most surprising?

5

Find the following words or expressions in the passages. Can you guess their meaning from the context?

a shock to the system
take it out on
on-channel
encroach

deaden the effect
flattering
compensates

Check your answers in a dictionary.

6

Complete the chart below.

	Sheila	*Lynn*	*George*	*Tony*
Occupation				
Reasons for loneliness				
How they coped with loneliness				

7

Do you think more people are lonely nowadays than ever before? Why? Look at the groups of people in Exercise 2 again. Write down some things they can do to help cope with their loneliness.

10 | How would you like to spend the night with him?

1 Look quickly at the passage on page 38 and decide if its intention is:

a) to describe how the homeless live;
b) to attract people to join the police force.

Where would you expect to find it?

2 Read the first part of the passage and decide who *you* refers to.

HOW WOULD YOU LIKE TO SPEND THE NIGHT WITH HIM?

It is a cold night on the beat. You're walking a part of London tourists will never see. On the left, waste ground strewn with rubbish leads into an alley lined with derelict warehouses.

Suddenly your eye is caught by a flickering light inside one of the buildings. Going closer, you see a small fire burning amidst a jumble of rubble and charred beams.

By the fire is a heap of rags which, as you approach, sits up and becomes a small man with matted hair.

At ten paces you can smell the drink on him. His trousers are held up by a piece of string, spittle drools onto his beard and you know that his clothes are probably heaving with lice and fleas.

The fire must be extinguished since it is a hazard. But what of this old man? What are you to do with him?

Move him on? But he has no family, no money and nowhere to go on this freezing night.

Arrest him for vagrancy? Section 4 of the Vagrancy Act (passed in 1824 to curb the excesses of ex-soldiers returning from the Napoleonic Wars) entitles you to consider as a rogue and vagabond any 'person wandering abroad and lodging in any deserted building and not giving a good account of himself...'

But is a night's lodging in a police cell and an appearance before a magistrate really the answer?

Try this. Before you kick the fire out, sit down and have a chat with him. Ask who he is and how he is and how he comes to be there.

You might be surprised. Vagrants are no easier to typecast than any other bunch of people. He may

have known no other life or led a normal existence until drink, disaster or other pressures overtook him.

He may be highly intelligent and well educated, contented or miserable.

One old man who has spent thirty years tramping the streets of London told us he was lonely because he had never made a friend. Can you imagine what it is like to be lonely for 30 years?

Ask if he is ill, or in need of any other help. You may be able to get him medical attention, or direct him to a soup kitchen where he will get a hot meal, or help him find a bed for the night. Help him and, who knows, another time he may even help you. He's on the street all the time and sees things that other people miss. He too may have his share of civic pride.

3 Answer the questions:

1 Which sentences describe a part of the town? What sort of area is it?
2 Which sentences describe the old man's physical appearance?
3 The old man can be arrested for vagrancy. What do you think *vagrancy* is?
4 *But is a night's lodging in a police cell and an appearance before a magistrate really the answer?* What is the answer suggested in the passage?

4 Read the next part of the passage and see if your ideas in Exercise 2 are confirmed.

However, the reason you help this old man is not because you stand to gain anything by it, but because as a police officer your job is to make yourself friendly and helpful to everyone you meet.

What kind of policing is this?

It certainly contradicts the view that the police exist solely to enforce law and order. We have always spent most of our time dealing with ordinary people and looking after their problems.

But over the last few years we have felt that technology – and particularly the police car – have created a distance between us and the community.

What we call 'community policing' is an attempt to get close to people again. It means focusing our attention on the 90% of people who never commit a crime, not just the 10% who break the law. Detecting and arresting criminals, yes, but also denying them opportunities and working harder to help their victims.

It means being useful to people in every way we can. Helping someone who is locked out of their flat. Looking out for old people whom we know to be living alone. (Taking this duty upon yourself may spare you the nastier one of forcing an entry to find a corpse.)

We'd expect you to get to know the people on your ground. Their youngsters. Their worries and problems.

When you've earned their trust and respect, you will find that their anger at crime is your most powerful weapon against criminals.

In areas which have had community policing for some years, the level of street crime has fallen, thanks to a concerned public and local council.

5 Find the sentences which explain the characteristics of 'community policing'. In what way does it differ from the general view of the police's functions?

What are the advantages of this kind of policing?

6 Make a list of the qualities and qualifications you think are needed to become a community police officer.

7 Read the rest of the passage and see if you agree with the advertisement.

... Does this interest you?

Maybe you would rather investigate robberies, or become a traffic officer, or trace frauds. These options will always be there, but today more than ever we need people who can appreciate the role of the police as a caring profession, working in the community.

It's not an easy job being a police officer and not everyone can do it. Five out of six people who apply will be turned down.

If you succeed you will undergo 20 weeks of physical and mental training at Hendon. Followed by 10 weeks of practical street duty instruction at one of London's many police stations.

Then it's out on the beat with just your radio for company. (Don't worry, the more senior colleagues will keep a watchful eye on you, and your formal training will continue.)

For the rest of your first two years you will be a probationer learning what only experience can teach you.

If you think you're what we're looking for, please fill and post the coupon below. You should be fit, aged between 18 and 45, at least 172cms tall if you're a man, 162cms if you're a woman.

We would especially like to see more candidates from the ethnic minorities.

We will be looking for some 'O' level passes or their equivalents, but as you will have gathered, your personal qualities are just as important.

8 Do you find this advertisement for police officers surprising? Do you think it is a realistic image of police work? Does this advertisement seem to you to be effective? Does it make you want to become a police officer?

9 What are the police like in your country? Are they respected and trusted by the general public? What would an advertisement for police officers in your country say?

11 | How well do you travel?

1 What is your idea of a successful holiday? Write down five things which are important for the success of your holiday.

Have you ever had a disappointing holiday? Can you explain why it was not successful?

2 The newspaper article which follows discusses some of the reasons why a holiday may be a failure. Read the article and decide which of these statements the writer would agree with.

1 A good holiday means a complete change of lifestyle.
2 The further you travel, the more fun you are likely to have.
3 A good holiday does not necessarily mean you have to do a lot.
4 It is important to be sure that your choice of holiday suits your needs.
5 It is not a good idea to travel too far from home.

MOST PEOPLE manage to return from their holidays with a wallet full of happy-snaps and a couple of amusing anecdotes. Not many will admit they've had a bad time.

But very few holiday-makers return without at least a private grievance or two. Leaving aside genuine matters of complaint – over-booked airlines, shoddy hotels, tacky resorts – most people who suffer bad holidays have only themselves to blame. Almost always, they have failed to match their destination, or type of holiday, close enough with their family's needs.

Of course it is part of the joy of planning a holiday that it promises a complete break from everyday routine. But you shouldn't fall into the trap of seeing this as some kind of annual metamorphosis, obliging you to pursue all sorts of activities which at home you would firmly avoid.

Why, for instance, does the philistine who never sets a weekend foot inside a British museum inexplicably feel compelled to visit a succession of Romanesque churches instead of more honestly enjoying a lazy day on the beach? How come the 40-fag-a-day sedentary lifestyler suddenly feels fit enough to handle a hiking, cross-country skiing or scuba-diving holiday?

An early American travel brochure once advertised a Caribbean holiday by telling prospective clients that they would visit eight islands in 10 days and 'fly real low over four others'. Over-ambitious schedules are another common cause of disappointment. Never lose sight of geographical realities. When studying the atlas, for instance, the whole of Australia may look manageable in a two-week whip-round. The lunacy of the enterprise becomes apparent only when you realise, say, that Perth is nearer to Singapore than it is to Sydney.

Such holidays are every bit as daft as they sound, but not as uncommon as you might think. In recent years travel companies have succeeded in selling us the idea that the further we go, the better our holiday will be. Do not be seduced. Why travel halfway round the globe when all you really want from your summer holiday can be had close by? Nowhere in the world has a better summer climate than the Mediterranean, so why pay more if all you want to do is swim and lie in the sun?

3 Read the article again and write down any difficult nouns or adjectives. Can you guess their meaning from the context?

4 Here are the definitions, in the context of the article, of some difficult nouns and adjectives. Do any of these definitions match the words you chose in Exercise 3?

photographs
complaint
a complete transformation or change
someone who is not interested in cultural visits
cigarette
a quick tour
madness
ridiculous

Can you match the definitions with words in the article?

5 Some people are good travellers and others are never satisfied. Do the following questionnaire and check your score.

QUESTIONNAIRE

1 **There is no sign of your luggage when you arrive at your destination in the middle of the night. Do you:**
   a) think what a terrible start to the holiday and decide to stay at the airport until it turns up?
   b) take a telephone number and ring back in the morning?
   c) do nothing and wait for the courier to sort things out?
   d) grab a taxi and tell the driver to take you to the nearest bar?

2 **At the hotel you are shown a room which has neither the balcony nor the sea view for which you've asked and paid. Do you:**
   a) take what you're offered for the moment, but determine to get what you want in the morning?
   b) refuse to accept the room and camp in the lounge?
   c) smile knowingly and turn up the volume on your Walkman (you knew things would go wrong)?
   d) take the room, certain you'll be able to swap?

3 **The bar at your hotel turns out to be ridiculously expensive. Do you:**
   a) drink without flinching, because there must be some way to get it off tax?
   b) pay up, but moan non-stop?
   c) decide to give up drinking for the duration?
   d) find a cheaper bar a couple of streets away?

4 **The weather is lousy. Do you:**
   a) see if there's any chance of an earlier flight home?
   b) stay in your room and listen to the Walkman?
   c) organise trips to museums and galleries until it gets better?
   d) make for the beach anyway? (You once read an article that said the sun can tan you even through thick clouds.)

5 **You go on a whole-day coach trip with regular stops for drinks, meals and sightseeing. The rest of the party don't look like the sort of people you'd mix with at home. Do you:**
   a) talk only to your holiday companion and thank God you both brought books?
   b) bitterly regret your mistake and spend the whole day in a huff?
   c) identify anyone who looks remotely congenial and see if you can engage them in conversation?
   d) make yourself the life and soul of the party?

6 **When you go away on holidays, do you:**
   a) hardly think about what's going on at home from the moment you leave until the moment you return?
   b) know there is absolutely no point in worrying about not having finished the project you were working on before you came away because someone else is bound to have coped with it?
   c) wake up most mornings worrying about how on earth they're coping without you?
   d) send postcards to a few close friends, but not until the second week of the holiday?

Key ⋙→

KEY

Each answer is awarded a key letter. For question 1, note down the letter Z if you chose answer (a), W if you chose (b), X if you chose (c), Y if you chose (d). Then treat the other questions in the same way:

2 (a)W, (b)Z, (c)Y, (d)X
3 (a)X, (b)Z, (c)Y, (d)W
4 (a)Z, (b)Y, (c)W, (d)X
5 (a)Y, (b)Z, (c)W, (d)X
6 (a)Y, (b)X, (c)Z, (d)W

There are at least four different ways of behaving on holiday, and most people display elements of more than one. Each of us, however, has a particular tendency.

If your answers have a predominance of W options, it shows you are a Good Holiday Person – flexible, adaptable and capable of improvisation in difficult situations, everyone's ideal companion.

A predominance of X answers reveals a Blind Optimist – given the right breaks, your blindness to reality may see you through, though you tend to be a very wearying holiday companion.

A majority of Ys indicates a Selfish Hedonist – determined to carry on with what you want to do, irrespective of what's happening around you. While you are capable of having a good time on even the most calamitous of holidays, you do not contribute to anyone else's enjoyment.

If Z answers predominate, you are an Autodestructive Grumbler – seeing trouble where none exists, and biting off your nose to spite your face.

---

6 **Answer the questions about the expressions *in italics*:**

1 There is *no sign of* your luggage. Does this mean that you did not put a name sticker on it; that you do not know where it is; or that somebody else has taken it?

2 The courier will *sort things out*. What do you want the courier to do about your luggage?

3 If you spend the day *in a huff*, are you likely to have a pleasant day with the others or to have a miserable time alone?

4 Is someone who is *the life and soul of the party* a pleasant person to be with or a very uncommunicative person?

5 Someone else *is bound* to have coped with the project. Is someone else likely or unlikely to have taken care of it?

7 **Write two more questions to continue the questionnaire. Here are some ideas:**

When checking how much money you have at the end of the first day, you realise you handed over a 2,000 instead of a 200 denomination note for lunch.

Having tried all the restaurants you are forced to acknowledge that the local cuisine is awful.

When you arrive at the beach, you find it is filthy and covered in tar.

The police have taken away your illegally-parked hired car. You don't speak the local language very well, but eventually you realise you're being asked to accompany them to the police station.

12 | Homesickness

1 **Do you enjoy being away from home? What do you miss most when you are away? Have you ever felt homesick? Why?**

2 **The passage on page 46 is from *The Independent*, which has a regular series of interviews with people talking about their best and worst times. Here, Dai Llewellyn relates his worst experience of homesickness. Read the passage and decide the main reason why he was unhappy. Was it because:**

- he wanted to go home?
- his grandmother was ill?
- he didn't like being alone in a foreign country?
- he wasn't spending Christmas with his family and friends?
- he couldn't stay at his grandmother's house?
- the hotel where he was staying was fifth class?

I munched my hamburger, alone on Christmas Day

The Christmas of 1979, I was visiting some friends in Rhodesia, and I decided not to go straight back to England, but to spend Christmas at my grandparents' home. My grandfather, an old boy called Lord de Saumarez, had just died, and I was going to stay with my grandmother, Lady de Saumarez. I rented a car at Cape Town airport, and drove off to the house, which is about 200 miles away on the southernmost tip of South Africa.

As I got to Berdasdorp, the nearest large town, I was almost knocked over by an ambulance going in the other direction at great speed.

I decided to freshen up a little in the local bar and I rang the house to say 'Hello' and that I'd be with them in about three-quarters of an hour – only to have the reply: 'I'm terribly sorry, but her ladyship's been taken to hospital in Cape Town.' In other words, in the ambulance I'd just seen was Grandma.

So I couldn't exactly stay in the house, which was called Springfield and had 11 miles of coastland and was incredibly beautiful and comfortable. I was looking forward to it. So I whacked back into Cape Town, two days before Christmas, to find every hotel full, and I eventually found one in Sea Point, which is a sort of beach suburb.

This hotel was very much fifth class – not five stars – and I can still remember the cracks on the ceiling. I couldn't sleep, I just tossed round and looked at the ceiling. When I stood at the bar, people stared at me . . . what was this man doing all on his own at Christmas? Probably lots of cheap South African brandy didn't help my morose state.

Everybody in the hotel was having a family Christmas, having a jolly time, and laughing and singing. It made me feel more and more isolated the longer it went on. I actually got myself into a really dark and terrible depression.

Going to see my grandmother was the high point of my day. Clomping wearily down the hospital passages: 'Hello, Grandma.'

'Err . . .'

'Isn't it a nice day?'

'. . . glugg . . .'

'Well, I'll go back to the hotel now . . .' Grandma wasn't making much sense. Visits lasted about half an hour, and after I'd paid my respects, I went back to the hotel to try and occupy myself.

It was just frightful, I was completely and utterly alone, it was the most miserable thing ever.

And then on Christmas Day itself, I was driving my rent-a-car from the hospital back to my dreadful hotel, back to the cracks in the ceiling, when the King's College choir came out with 'Hark the Herald Angels Sing' on the wireless of my rent-a-car . . . and before I knew where I was, on a bright and very hot sunny day, I was in a flood of tears and had to pull the car over to the side of the road, feeling incredibly sorry for myself, and incredibly alone at Christmas.

It was somehow all the worse because it was hot, with everybody running around on beaches, having a great time. If I had been a complete down-and-out underneath Waterloo Bridge, I somehow wouldn't have minded if it was cold – but I love the cold, and I love Christmas. I'm a terribly Christmas person. I used to train the local choir, and Midnight Mass at our local church is just an incredibly special and wonderful time . . .

I think the worst time was Christmas lunch: all the hotels were having their 'Christmas lunch', but I didn't want to have it all on my own, so I went to a hamburger stand, and I had this filthy, greasy hamburger, and that was my Christmas lunch, off the back of a truck in a car park on Sea Point, and I sat in the car and munched away at this repulsive hamburger, alone on Christmas Day.

3 Complete the following sentences with explanations from the passage:

    1 He couldn't stay at Springfield because ....
    2 He couldn't stay in Cape Town because ....
    3 He drank lots of cheap brandy because ....
    4 He had to stop the car because ....
    5 He didn't have Christmas lunch at the hotel because ....

4 What words or expressions does the writer use to describe:

    – Springfield?
    – the hotel?
    – the hamburger?

Do you think the writer describes these things as they really were or the way he saw them at the time?

What words or expressions does he use to describe his feelings? How does he describe people around him? What is the effect of this contrast?

5 The writer uses a number of strong adverbs in the passage.

Example: (I was) feeling *incredibly* sorry for myself ...

Find some more examples. What effect do they have?

6 Answer the questions:

    1 What is he saying about his day when he writes: *Going to see my grandmother was the high point of my day*?
    2 Why did he cry when he heard the choir singing 'Hark the Herald Angels Sing' on the radio?
    3 Why was it *somehow all the worse because it was hot*?

7 Do you sympathise with the writer? Or do you think he was indulging in self-pity? If so, can you explain what words or sentences give this impression?

What do you think about his attitude to his grandmother?

8 Have you ever had a similar experience of homesickness? Is there a particular time of year when you would not like to be away from home?

13 | American dreams decoded

1 What ideas do you associate with the 'American dream'? Do you think it still exists today?

2 The writer of the newspaper articles in this unit has chosen two topics to illustrate how the American dream still persists today. Look quickly at the articles and find out what these topics are.

3 Read the first article, on page 49, and decide which paragraphs:

a) describe characteristics of the American way of life?
b) analyse these characteristics?

4 In each of these sentences from the first article there is a word missing. Without looking back at the article, try and find suitable words to fill the blanks.

a) '...while indoors, you can wear clothes which are the exact opposite of those .... for the season.'
b) 'If it's .... outside and you can actually watch the grass turning brown on the lawn, then you should be comfortable in a thick woollen sweater.'
c) 'In winter, department stores sometimes arrange for a curtain of air so hot you can see it .... from above the front door to street level.'
d) 'I suspect it's connected to the basic American .... that there might not be enough.'

Now look at the article again. Did you choose the same words? Do you understand the words in the article? You can use your dictionary to check.

The modern American home has come to a unique temperature arrangement. During the summer in say, the Midwest, the temperature outside may be 100 degrees F. But inside it is freezing, like a meat store. In winter, the temperature can be 30 degrees below zero, but indoors it's up to 80 degrees.

The general idea is that a home is at the right temperature if, while indoors, you can wear clothes which are the exact opposite of those appropriate for the season. If it's freezing outside, you should be able to wear a T-shirt and shorts in the house. If it's sweltering outside and you can actually watch the grass turning brown on the lawn, then you should be comfortable in a thick woollen sweater.

In winter, department stores sometimes arrange for a curtain of air so hot you can see it blast from above the front door to street level. Go from the cold outside across this curtain once or twice, and you can recreate exactly how a kebab feels on a spit. Inside the store it's fractionally more temperate, but the message is the same: 'We're not mean, look, we'll keep you warmer than you could ever need!'

This obsession with inverting the temperature tells us, I think, something about the United States. I suspect it's connected to the basic American dread that there might not be enough. America is a huge country, but in more than just acreage; so much inside it is vast as well. It has to be, otherwise you would have this fear that it might not be enough, that you might run out.

For the people who came to this abundant continent, and their descendants today, it was not enough to have escaped poverty and hunger; they had to put as great a distance between it and them as they possibly could. Of course there are many poor people in the United States, and they are visible on every corner in the centre of most big cities. But they, too, share the American dream: one day they will have more – far more – than enough of everything, including food and heat.

5 Answer the questions:

1 What is the 'unique temperature arrangement'?
2 Which sentence implies that stores are overheated?
3 What does the writer suggest is the real reason for overheating in stores?
4 How does the writer define the American dream?

6

Read the next article. Find the sentences which express general statements about the American attitude to shopping.

What examples does the writer choose to illustrate these statements?

1 Americans are fascinated by their own love of shopping. This does not make them unique. It's just that they have more to buy than most other people on the planet. It's also an affirmation of faith in their country, its prosperity and limitless bounty. They have shops the way that lesser countries have statues. When the superlative Union Station was rebuilt in Washington, what did they choose to stuff it with? Dozens of shops, of course. They're the first thing many visitors see when they arrive in the nation's capital, proud symbols of America's majesty. The Capitol is what you see next.

Shopping is done at the mall. A typical mall coves an area roughly the size of Liechtenstein, and has nearly as many stores. Food stores are among the glories of America. The most stupendous grocery I have ever seen was the Safeway in Page, Arizona. Page is a small town in the middle of the desert, sur-

2 rounded by millions of acres of scrub and sand. The Page Safeway has cereal shelves the length of a football field. Ninety-seven different types of yoghurt. More French wines than you would expect in a French supermarket. Heaps of fresh seafood a thousand miles from the sea. Vast dizzying towers of produce, cliffs of oranges, embankments of melons, escarpments of asparagus, all kept fresh and crisp in 110 degree temperatures by means of remorseless air-conditioning.

3 All around the world people live in deserts, and they expect to adapt their lives accordingly. They live in tents so they can move easily to where the water is. They conserve food and liquids. They have a limited diet. America is the only country in the world where desert dwellers believe they have the right to live precisely as if they inhabited the centre of a large temperate city.

7

Read the last paragraph again. What is the writer implying? Choose from the following statements:

a) Americans are the only people in the world who have everything they want.
b) In other parts of the world, people who live in deserts have to adapt themselves to their environment.
c) Americans believe that they don't have to adapt to their environment.
d) Americans believe that they have a right to everything their country has to offer no matter where they live.

8 What do the words *in italics* in the following phrases have in common? What effect do they have?

> *vast dizzying towers* of produce
> *cliffs* of oranges
> *embankments* of melons
> *escarpments* of asparagus

How do you feel about the aspects of the American way of life that are described in the articles? Would you say that the writer exaggerates?

9 How does life in America compare with life in your country? Do you feel attracted to the American lifestyle? Write a paragraph comparing America with your country. You may like to use the articles as a model.

14 | The aqueduct

1 The passage in this unit is a short story called *The Aqueduct* by Ray Bradbury, a popular American contemporary writer. Before you read the story, think about the answers to these questions about aqueducts.

> What do they look like?
> What are they made of?
> Where do you find them?
> When and why were they built?
> Who built them?

2 *The Aqueduct* is an allegory. Read the story, on page 53, and choose the best definition.

> An allegory: a) has a plot which can be taken at face value;
> b) has a plot which is a pretext to say something else.

3 What do you think the story is about?

- international cooperation
- the fear of war
- the importance of water
- survival at the expense of others
- solidarity between nations
- human society
- human rights

Did you enjoy the story? Did anything shock you? If so, can you say why?

4 How do the people in the South react to the news about the war in the North?

What effect does the war in the North have on the life of people in the South? How do we know?

The Aqueduct

It leapt over the country in great stone arches. It was empty now, with the wind blowing in its sluices; it took a year to build, from the land in the North to the land in the South.

'Soon,' said mothers to their children, 'soon now the Aqueduct will be finished. Then they will open the gates a thousand miles North and cool water will flow to us, for our crops, our flowers, our baths, and our tables.'

The children watched the Aqueduct being built stone on solid stone. It towered thirty feet in the sky, with great gargoyle spouts every hundred yards which would drop tiny streams down into yard reservoirs.

In the North there was not only one country, but two. They had rattled their sabres and clashed their shields for many years.

Now, in the Year of the Finishing of the Aqueduct, the two Northern countries shot a million arrows at each other and raised a million shields, like numerous suns, flashing.

At the year's end the Aqueduct stood finished. The people of the Hot South, waiting, asked, 'When will the water come? With war in the North, will we starve for water, will our crops die?'

A courier came racing. 'The war is terrible,' he said. 'There is a slaughtering that is unbelievable. More than one hundred million people have been slain.'

'For what?'

'They disagreed, those two Northern countries.'

'That's all we know. They disagreed.'

The people gathered all along the stone Aqueduct. Messengers ran along the empty sluiceways with yellow streamers, crying, 'Bring vases and bowls, ready your fields and ploughs, open your baths, fetch water glasses!'

A thousand miles of filling Aqueduct and the slap of naked courier feet in the channel, running ahead. The people gathered by the tens of millions from the boiling countryside, the sluiceways open, waiting, their crocks, urns, jugs, held towards the gargoyle spouts where the wind whistled emptily.

'It's coming!' The word passed from person to person down the one thousand miles.

And from a great distance, there was the sound of rushing and running, the sound that liquid makes in a stone channel. It flowed slowly at first and then faster, and then very fast down into the Southern land, under the hot sun.

'It's here! Any second now. Listen!' said the people. They raised their glasses into the air.

Liquid poured from the sluiceways down the land, out of gargoyle mouths, into the stone baths, into the glasses, into the fields. The fields were made rich for the harvest. People bathed. There was a singing you could hear from one field to one town to another.

'But, Mother!' A child held up his glass and shook it, the liquid whirled slowly. 'This isn't water!'

'Hush!' said the mother.

'It's red,' said the child. 'And it's thick.'

'Here's the soap, wash yourself, don't ask questions, shut up,' she said. 'Hurry into the field, open the sluicegates, plant the rice!'

In the fields, the father and his two sons laughed into one another's faces. 'If this keeps up, we've a great life ahead. A full silo and a clean body.'

'Don't worry,' said the two sons. 'The President is sending a representative North to make certain that the two countries there continue to disagree.'

'Who knows, it might be a fifty-year war!'

They sang and smiled.

And at night they all lay happily, listening to the good sound of the Aqueduct, full and rich, like a river, rushing through their land towards the morning.

5 Answer the questions:

1 When is the story set? Which words in the story helped you decide? Is the time setting important?
2 What role do the children play in the story?
3 What effect does the use of capital letters have when referring to the North and the South, and the Year of the Finishing of the Aqueduct?
4 Would you say the writer uses a 'personal' or an 'impersonal' style? What effect does this have?
5 The first part of the story builds up to a climax when the liquid finally pours through the sluiceways of the Aqueduct. Find words or sentences which increase the tension of expectation.
6 *'More than one hundred million people have been slain'* because the two countries *'disagreed'*. What is surprising about these statements? What idea do they convey?
7 *'It's red,' said the child. 'And it's thick.'* What is the effect of these words? Why are they important for our interpretation of the story?

6 Does *The Aqueduct* remind you of any situations in the world today? If the story were to be set in modern times, what changes would have to be made? Would an aqueduct be a suitable choice for a modern *allegory* or can you think of something different?

7 Do you agree with the writer's view of life and society? Do you think he is realistic or over-pessimistic?

15 | Traveler

1 In this unit, the writer of the article *Traveler* is Garrison Keillor, who was born in Minnesota in 1942. He is famous for his articles and radio programmes in which he describes life and recent events in the town of Lake Wobegon, deep in the heart of Middle America.

Read the last sentence of *Traveler* and try to guess what the article is about.

> The night when your child returns with dust on his shoes from a country you've never seen is a night you would gladly prolong into a week.

2 Read *Traveler* on page 56, and find out if you were right. What information does it reveal about the writer?

3 Decide which of these statements accurately reflect the writer's feelings.

1 He's fascinated by places he's heard of but has never visited.
2 He's disappointed that he never had the experiences he had intended by the age of twenty-one.
3 He's very over-protective about his son.
4 He's extremely proud of his son.
5 He's very upset that his son dresses badly.

4 Look at this summary of the article. Do you think it leaves out any of the main points?

Keillor's son has just returned from his first visit to Europe with relatives. The advice Keillor gave his son was not useful, as Keillor has never visited these countries. Keillor is amazed by his son's news and by the fact that the son has done something he has never done himself.

Is there any essential information you would like to add or change?

Traveler

My fifteen-year-old son has just returned from abroad with a dozen rolls of exposed film and a hundred dollars in uncashed traveler's checks, and is asleep at the moment, drifting slowly westward toward Central Time. His blue duffel bag lies on the hall floor where he dropped it, about four short strides into the house. Last night, he slept in Paris, and the twenty nights before that in various beds in England and Scotland, but evidently he postponed as much sleep as he could: when he walked in and we embraced and he said he'd missed home, his electrical system suddenly switched off, and he headed half-unconscious for the sack, where I imagine he beat his old record of sixteen hours.

I don't think I'll sleep for a while. This household has been running a low fever over the trip since weeks before it began, when we said, 'In one month, you'll be in London! Imagine!' It was his first trip overseas, so we pressed travel books on him, and a tape cassette of useful French phrases; drew up a list of people to visit; advised him on clothing and other things. At the luggage store where we went to buy him a suitcase, he looked at a few suitcases and headed for the duffels and knapsacks. He said that suitcases were more for old people. I am only in my forties, however, and I pointed out that a suitcase keeps your clothes neater – a sports coat, for example. He said he wasn't taking a sports coat. The voice of my mother spoke through me. 'Don't you want to look nice?' I said. He winced in pain and turned away.

My mother and father and a nephew went with him on the trip, during which he called home three times: from London, from Paris, and from a village named Ullapool, in the Highlands. 'It's like no place in America,' he reported from London. Near Ullapool, he hiked through a crowd of Scottish sheep and climbed a mountain in a rainstorm that almost blew him off the summit. He took cover behind a boulder, and the sun came out. In the village, a man spoke to him in Gaelic, and, too polite to interrupt, my son listened to him for ten or fifteen minutes, trying to nod and murmur in the right places. The French he learned from the cassette didn't hold water in Paris – not even his fallback phrase, *'Parlez-vous anglais?'* The French he said it to shrugged and walked on. In Paris, he bought a hamburger at a tiny shop run by a Greek couple, who offered Thousand Island dressing in place of ketchup. He described Notre Dame to me, and the Eiffel Tower, as he had described Edinburgh, Blair Castle, hotel rooms, meals, people he saw on the streets.

'What's it like?' I asked over and over. I myself have never been outside the United States, except twice when I was in Canada. When I was eighteen, a friend and I made a list of experiences we intended to have before we reached twenty-one, which included hopping a freight to the West Coast, learning to play the guitar, and going to Europe. I've done none of them. When my son called, I sat down at the kitchen table and leaned forward and hung on every word. His voice came through clearly, though two of the calls were like ship-to-shore communication in which you have to switch from Receive to Send, and when I interrupted him with a 'Great!' or a 'Really?' I knocked a little hole in his transmission. So I just sat and listened. I have never listened to a telephone so intently and with so much pleasure as I did those three times. It was wonderful and moving to hear news from him that was so new to me. In my book, he was the first man to land on the moon, and I knew that I had no advice to give him and that what I had already given was probably not much help.

The unused checks that he's left on the hall table – almost half the wad I sent him off with – is certainly evidence of that. Youth travels light. No suitcase, no sports coat, not much language, and a slim expense account, and yet he went to the scene, got the story, and came back safely. I sit here amazed. The night when your child returns with dust on his shoes from a country you've never seen is a night you would gladly prolong into a week.

5 Look at this sentence from the article:

> In the village, a man spoke to him in Gaelic, and, too polite to interrupt, my son listened to him for ten or fifteen minutes, trying to nod and murmur in the right places.

Find three more details or items of extra information and decide which you find most effective.

6 Another feature of the article is the images and similes the writer uses. What do you think he means by the following?

1 ... drifting slowly westward toward Central Time.
2 ... his electrical system suddenly switched off ...
3 ... he was the first man to land on the moon ...

Can you find any other images and similes? Can you work out what they mean?

7 One of the strongest features of the article is the writer's love for and pride in his son. For example:

> When my son called, I sat down at the kitchen table and leaned forward and hung on every word.

Can you find other examples?

8 Think of somewhere you would like to visit. If you couldn't go there yourself, who would you ask to go there for you?

9 Can you think of a particular occasion when you became independent from your parents? If you have children, have they reached this stage yet? Write a paragraph describing what happened. You may like to use the article as a model.

16 | Accidental discoveries

'In the fields of observation, chance favours only the prepared mind.'

Louis Pasteur

Many things which make everyday living more convenient, pleasant, healthy or interesting were discovered by accident. The passages in this unit describe the fortuitous accidents that have resulted in some surprising discoveries.

1

Match the following people with their discoveries.

Nobel   Newton   Pasteur
Becquerel   Curie   Mackintosh

a) ... formulated laws relating to gravity and motion.
b) ... discovered the element radium.
c) ... discovered dynamite.
d) ... invented a waterproof raincoat made of rubberised cloth.
e) ... discovered a process to destroy harmful micro-organisms in certain types of food by heating.
f) ... devised a way of measuring radioactivity.

2

You are going to read passages about the following:

Post-its   Pluto   penicillin   the Lascaux caves

Before you read the passages, write down anything you know about the discoveries.

3

Read passage A on page 60, and answer the questions:

What are Post-its?
What are they for?
What were they first used for?
Where do you find them?

A People who use the usually yellow but possibly any-other-color self-sticking notes can't imagine what they did before without them. These ubiquitous slips of paper are found in offices on letters and file folders, by telephones and computer screens, in homes on the refrigerator and the TV screen, or possibly by the back door. These notes which were invented at 3M and named Post-its have since been imitated and sold by everyone else.

In 1974 Art Fry was employed by the 3M company in product development. On Sundays he sang in the church choir. He marked his choir book with scraps of paper, to facilitate finding the proper music quickly at the proper time in the second service. But sometimes the scraps fell out without warning, causing Fry to scramble through the pages.

'I don't know if it was a dull sermon or divine inspiration,' says Fry, 'but my mind began to wander and suddenly I thought of an adhesive that had been discovered several years earlier by another 3M scientist, Dr Spencer Silver.' Spencer had discarded the adhesive, Fry remembered, because it was not strong enough to be permanently useful. Fry's inspiration was that this adhesive might serve to keep his place temporarily in the choir book without the marker becoming permanently attached – a 'temporarily permanent adhesive', as Fry put it.

The rest is history. In 1980 Post-its were widely used throughout the United States, and by early 1981 sales in Europe paralleled those in the United States.

4 Read passage B and put these notes in the right order.

a) technician came
b) found other photos
c) noticed a bulge on photo
d) further studies
e) looked carefully at photo
f) measuring Pluto's orbit
g) stayed to help
h) looked through archives
i) machine stopped working
j) using Star Scan
k) became interested
l) thought it was an error

B An accident led to this important discovery by James Christy at the U.S. Naval Observatory in 1978. Christy was measuring the orbital characteristics of Pluto. To do so, he had placed a photographic plate containing a picture of Pluto on an instrument called a Star Scan machine. When he did so, he noticed an elongation of the image of the planet. At first he assumed the bulge was an artifact and was going to discard the photograph. Luckily, however (as it turned out), the machine began to malfunction at that instant. Christy called in an electronics technician to repair the machine. The technician asked Christy to stand by while he made the repairs, because he thought he might need Christy's help.

During the hour required for the repair, Christy studied the photograph more carefully, and as a result he decided to look through the archives for earlier pictures of the planet. The first one he found was marked 'Pluto image. Elongated. Plate no good. Reject.' His interest now aroused, Christy searched through the archives and found six more pictures dated between 1965 and 1970 that showed the same bulge. His further studies proved that the bulge was a moon of the planet. If the Star Scan machine had not broken down when it did, he would not have discovered the new moon.

5 **Check you understand the meaning of the following words. You can use a dictionary.**

> antibiotic   bacteria   culture   a cold   influenza   germ
> mould   cells

Now read passage C and complete the following notes about Fleming's discovery.

> caught a cold
> ………………
> a tear fell on to the culture
> noticed clear area in culture
> called substance lysozyme
> ………………
> ………………
> made cultures in petri dishes
> ………………
> mould fell into dish
> noticed clear area in culture
> thought of previous discovery
> ………………
> called substance penicillin

C Perhaps one of the best-known accidental discoveries is Sir Alexander Fleming's discovery of penicillin. In 1922 Fleming accidentally discovered an antibiotic that killed bacteria but not white blood cells. While suffering from a cold, Fleming made a culture from some of his own nasal secretions. As he examined the culture dish, filled with yellow bacteria, a tear fell from his eye into the dish. The next day when he examined the culture, he found a clear space where the tear had fallen. His keen observation and inquisitiveness led him to the correct conclusion: the tear contained a substance that caused rapid destruction of the bacteria, but was harmless to human tissue. The antibiotic in the tear he named *lysozyme*. It turned out to be of little practical importance, because the germs that lysozyme killed were relatively harmless, but this discovery was an essential prelude to that of penicillin, as we shall see.

In 1928, Fleming was doing research on influenza. While carrying out some routine laboratory work that involved microscopic examination of cultures of bacteria grown in petri dishes (flat glass dishes with covers), Fleming noticed in one dish an unusual clear area. Examination showed that the clear area surrounded a spot where a bit of mould had fallen onto the dish, which had been left uncovered. Remembering his experience with lysozyme, Fleming concluded that the mould was producing something that was deadly to the Staphylococcus bacteria in the culture dish.

Fleming isolated the mould and identified it as belonging to the genus *Penicillium*, and he named the antibiotic substance it produced *penicillin*.

6 **Read passage D and write notes like the ones in Exercises 4 and 5.**

D   In 1940, four boys were exploring the woods near the town of Montignac in south-western France when they discovered a small hole in the ground. Curious, they enlarged the hole enough to crawl inside, and they found a narrow passage that led into a large underground cave. With the light of their oil lantern they were amazed to see brilliantly coloured paintings of animals on the white limestone walls and ceiling of the cave. They reported their discovery to their former schoolmaster, who made a telephone call to the Abbé Henri Breuil, an expert on prehistoric art. Breuil came to see the cave paintings and proclaimed them to be authentically ancient. When news of the discovery reached the public, archaeologists, journalists and sightseers came to the cave; they were admitted in small, carefully controlled groups. After the war the French government and the landowner provided a safer entrance and better security for the paintings. Since that time, thousands of tourists have come to Lascaux Cave. They can now view an exact replica that has been built adjacent to the original cave without danger of damaging the irreplaceable original artwork.

7 **Have you ever used or seen any of the four things in the passages? In your opinion, which of the discoveries is the most important? Which is the least important?**

8 **Think of a recent discovery or invention which has affected your life. Write a paragraph describing it. You may like to use the passages as a model.**

17 | Love and marriage

1 The poems in this unit are by Brian Patten and Edward Lucie-Smith, two contemporary British poets. They are about *love and marriage*. Write down five words which you would use if you were writing a poem on these subjects.

2 The poem *The Package* by Brian Patten is about a married couple. Read the poem. What can you say about their relationship?

The Package

At dinner, long-faced and miserable,
They cast sly glances at the other guests,
The pink-kneed husband and wife
Sitting with their five-year-old, complaining pest.
The holiday brochure they'd believed in, lied,
Still they blamed each other for the clouds
And ever since arriving they had rowed.

After dinner, the child put to bed,
They bickered beneath the hotel's vine
And the ghosts of false what-might-have-beens
Surfaced with each extra glass of wine.
Theirs was a package holiday all right;
     A package stuffed
With years of rootless longings and regrets.
Their bickering done, they sat mutely and both grieved
For what neither might have anyway achieved.

The next day they'd gone. They'd cut
Their holiday short, and carried back with them
A failure of another sort.
It was a failure to understand how all
Their arguments revolved around
An earlier package that they'd bought –
One promoted by both Church and State, one written
In the same tempting style; one over which
A watery sun shone the same short while.

Brian Patten

3 Answer the following questions:

1 Read stanza 1 again and write down three statements about the couple. Example: They are unhappy.

2 What do the words *in italics* make us think about the couple?
sly glances
pink-kneed husband
complaining pest
blamed each other

3 The couple regret the things they have not done. But the poem suggests that these regrets are only illusions. Which lines suggest that their regrets are illusions?

4 Read stanza 3 again and decide what the package holiday and the couple's marriage have in common.

4 How do you feel about the poem? Decide which of the following statements you agree or disagree with. Can you explain why?

I like the poem.
It is a harsh description of married life.
It is very pessimistic.
I don't like the poem.
It is very personal.
It is not meant to be a general statement about married life.
It is very depressing.
I'd like to read more poems by this poet.

5 Read *The Son* by Edward Lucie-Smith. What does it have in common with the first poem?

The Son

Lying awake, in the room
over their room, the voices
drifting up through the floor-boards –
a grinding, night-long quarrel
between the two who made you.
How can you bear to listen?

A shared bed, a shared hatred
to warm it in the small hours.
Four living children, one dead.
Five proofs of something, one you
who lie there above them. Grey
coals hiss as the fire burns low.

Edward Lucie-Smith

6 Answer the questions:

1 Who is lying awake?
2 Whose *voices* are *drifting up through the floor-boards*?
3 What do you think *something* refers to?
4 What do the metaphors in the line *Grey coals hiss as the fire burns low* refer to?

7 Look at the statements in Exercise 4 and think about *The Son*. Which statements would you agree or disagree with?

8 Do you believe in 'love for ever'? Do you think that the Western concept of 'romantic love' is an illusion encouraged by television and cinema? Do people have the same attitude to love and marriage in your country?

9 Here are two more poems on the same theme. Read them for your pleasure. You can use a dictionary to help you.

I Caught a Train That Passed the Town Where You Lived

I caught a train that passed the town where you lived
On the journey I thought of you.
One evening when the park was soaking
You hid beneath the trees, and all around you dimmed itself
as if the earth were lit by gaslight.
We had faith that love would last forever.

I caught a train that passed the town where you lived.

Brian Patten

The Cynic's only Love Poem

Love comes and goes
And often it has paused.
Then comes back to see
The damage it has caused.

Brian Patten

18 | Hospitality

1 This unit is about hospitality. Can you remember what was the most hospitable act you have ever experienced?

2 The passages in this unit describe hospitality in three countries. Read the passages and decide which countries they are.

A Hospitality is natural in my village. Guests arrive at any time of the day or night and they are always welcome. Nobody asks them 'Why have you come?' or 'How long are you going to stay?' They become a part of the family.

   The villagers are delighted to receive guests. They are fed, clothed and given presents. When guests arrive they are offered a pot of water to wash their hands, face and feet. Then they are given a mat or a chair to sit on. Previously, sherbet was offered, but now it is the custom to give a cup of tea, depending on the time of day. Guests are never asked 'Have you eaten?' or 'Would you like something to eat or drink?' Food is placed before them and it is impolite for guests to refuse. Hospitality is always disinterested and means giving yourself completely to guests and strangers.

B I was on my way to the Taiyetos Mountains. The sun was setting when my car broke down near a remote and poor village. Cursing my misfortune, I was wondering where I was going to spend the night when I realised that the villagers who had gathered around me were vehemently arguing as to who should have the honour of receiving me as a guest in their house. Finally, I accepted the offer of an old peasant woman who lived alone in a little house at the edge of the village. While she was getting me settled into a tiny but clean and freshly whitewashed room, the mayor of the village was hitching up his mule to my car to haul it to a small town some 20 kilometres away where there was a garage.

I had noticed three hens running free in my hostess's courtyard and that night one of them ended up in a stew on my table. Other villagers brought me goat's cheese, figs and honey, and, of course, some ouzo. I ate with a hearty appetite and, despite my ignorance of the language, we drank together and made merry till far into the night. The following day the garage man brought back my car which he had patched up.

When the time came for me to say goodbye to my friends in the village, I wanted to reward the old woman for the trouble to which I had put her and for the hen she had sacrificed for me. She refused the money I offered with cries of indignation. The more I insisted, the more vexed she appeared.

C Half Sweden had arrived on the ferry and not even the smallest broom-cupboard was available in any of the hotels. The tourist office – open at midnight – had compiled a list of addresses of families who had offered to put up visitors with nowhere to go.

I ended up at about one o'clock in the morning in the home of people who had risen from their beds, run me a bath and placed sandwiches on the table for me, to the accompaniment of great gestures of friendship – and all this without a word being exchanged, since they knew none of the languages in which I could manage a few stumbling phrases. I stayed with them for two days and, when the time came for me to leave, they got together a few friends to give a party in my honour, still communicating with sign language, since their friends were no better linguists than they were. They refused to let me pay for the room and I had to go back to the tourist office and leave the money there.

3 Decide which passage(s) is written from the 'guest' point of view, and which is written from the 'host' point of view.

4   Decide if the following are first or last paragraphs. Match them with the passages.

1   It is a religious act in India and a stranger should never leave the village displeased. Who knows, he may be the God Vishnu in disguise.

2   A Greek friend later explained to me that hospitality is part of a long tradition in Greece and is certainly not for sale. Even today, the Greek word 'xenos' means both 'foreigner' and 'guest'.

3   The most moving experience of hospitality I have ever had occurred in Copenhagen. I arrived there one Saturday, just before midnight, on the eve of a big football match between Malmö and Copenhagen.

5   A number of unexpected events happened to the writers of passages B and C. Read the passages again and say what they were.

Write down five similarities in the way the guests were treated in the two countries.

6   Read passage A again and choose four sentences from the passage which characterise hospitality in this Indian village.

7   How would you feel if you found yourself in the situations of the guests in the passages? How would you react?

8   Think about what a guest in your country would expect to experience. Write a paragraph describing typical customs of hospitality in your country. You may like to use the passages as a model.

19 | Mazes

1 The photos are of mazes built at different times and in different parts of the world. Read the texts below and match them with the photos. There is one extra photo.

a)

b)

1 The riddle of the maze reaches back several millennia, and is spread over many parts of the world. Remarkably, one archetypal labyrinth, the seven-ring design prevailed throughout the world. These early rock carvings may have symbolised the journey through life to death.

c)

2 An extraordinary craze for building mazes seized Japan in the 1980s when 200 wooden mazes were built within five years. These were often highly complex and three-dimensional, calculated to take 90 minutes to negotiate; some had time-clocks so that the competitive could log their progress.

d)

3 European hedge mazes were comparatively simple puzzles which provided a quarter of an hour's diversion in a private garden. Hampton Court Palace has probably the world's most famous hedge maze and the oldest in England. It was planted as part of the gardens laid out for William of Orange in 1690.

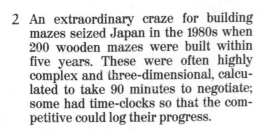

2 The passages which follow are from the novel *Three Men in a Boat* by
Jerome K. Jerome. The story is about three men and a dog who go on a
week's boating holiday on the river. This extract is an account of how one
of the men went into the Hampton Court maze to show his cousin the
way. Read the first part of the extract and answer the questions.

a) Is this maze likely to be large or small?
b) What has happened to the people?
c) Who is the main character in the passage?

> They met some people soon after they had got inside, who
> said they had been there for three-quarters of an hour, and
> had had about enough of it. Harris told them they could
> follow him, if they liked; he was just going in, and then
> should turn round and come out again. They said it was very
> kind of him, and fell behind, and followed.
>
> They picked up various other people who wanted to get it
> over, as they went along, until they had absorbed all the
> persons in the maze. People who had given up all hopes of
> ever getting either in or out, or of ever seeing their home
> and friends again, plucked up courage, at the sight of Harris
> and his party, and joined the procession, blessing him.
> Harris said he should judge there must have been twenty
> people following him, in all; and one woman with a baby,
> who had been there all the morning, insisted on taking his
> arm, for fear of losing him.

3 Read the first part again and decide who or what the words *in italics* refer
to.

They met some people ...
... soon after they had got *inside* ...
... had had about enough of *it*.
... who wanted to get *it* over ...
... insisted on taking *his* arm ...
... for fear of losing *him*.

4 How did the people feel:

– before they met Harris and his cousin?
– after they met Harris and his cousin?

Choose from this list of adjectives:

desperate   angry   frightened   fed up   confident
reassured   relieved   doubtful   worried   surprised   bored

5 Read the next part and decide if the same adjectives which you chose in
Exercise 4 can still be used to describe how the people felt.

Which sentences suggest that people are losing confidence in Harris?

> Harris kept on turning to the right, but it seemed a long way,
> and his cousin said he supposed it was a very big maze.
>   'Oh, one of the largest in Europe,' said Harris.
>   'Yes, it must be,' replied the cousin, 'because we've walked
> a good two miles already.'
>   Harris began to think it rather strange himself, but he held
> on until, at last, they passed the half of a penny bun on the
> ground that Harris's cousin swore he had noticed there
> seven minutes ago. Harris said: 'Oh, impossible!' but the
> woman with the baby said, 'Not at all,' as she herself had
> taken it from the child, and thrown it down there, just before
> she met Harris. She also added that she wished she never
> had met Harris, and expressed an opinion that he was an
> imposter. That made Harris mad, and he produced his map,
> and explained his theory.
>   'The map may be all right enough,' said one of the party,
> 'if you know whereabouts in it we are now.'

6 Read the last part (on the next page) and answer the questions.

1 What 'didn't Harris know'?
2 Why was Harris's suggestion of going back to the entrance and
   beginning again absurd?
3 What is the general attitude towards Harris now? Find two sentences
   which describe this attitude.
4 ... *curl his hair with it*. Is this likely to be a pleasant or an unpleasant
   suggestion?
5 Find another word in the passage which means 'crowd'.
6 How would you describe the tone of the passage?

Harris didn't know, and suggested that the best thing to do would be to go back to the entrance, and begin again. For the beginning again part of it there was not much enthusiasm; but with regard to the advisability of going back to the entrance there was complete unanimity, and so they turned, and trailed after Harris again, in the opposite direction. About ten minutes more passed, and then they found themselves in the centre.

Harris thought at first of pretending that that was what he had been aiming at; but the crowd looked dangerous, and he decided to treat it as an accident.

Anyhow, they had got something to start from then. They did know where they were, and the map was once more consulted, and the thing seemed simpler than ever, and off they started for the third time. And three minutes later they were back in the centre again.

After that they simply couldn't get anywhere else. Whatever way they turned brought them back to the middle. It became so regular at length, that some of the people stopped there, and waited for the others to take a walk round, and come back to them. Harris drew out his map again, after a while, but the sight of it only infuriated the mob, and they told him to go and curl his hair with it. Harris said that he couldn't help feeling that, to a certain extent, he had become unpopular . . .

7 How do you think they get out of the maze? Turn to page 85 of the *Answer key* to see if you guessed correctly.

8 Have you ever visited a maze? Are there any famous mazes in your country? Do you know any legends or stories about mazes?

20 | Crane diver

1   The story you are going to read is called *Crane Diver*, by the contemporary writer Valerie Thornton who lives in and writes about Glasgow. Before you read it, look at the photo of the city in which the story is set. Write down some words to describe your impressions. Would you like to live there?

Valerie Thornton

2 Read the first part of *Crane Diver* and write a sentence explaining what the crane diver did in the story.

Crane Diver

No one had ever believed him, that one summer evening he had wandered on to the docks, under the legs of the biggest crane, and climbed the steel ladder, up, up, and up into the swaying heights of the counterweights and control house.

The view over the city had been inspiring – the smoking derelict docklands, with miles of kingfisher-walled warehouses; the sun-tinted towers of distant churches; the cars, like insects, creeping one after the other along the expressway. Clinging to the drifting girders, he felt like the most successful man in the world.

He crawled, monkey-fashion, along the steel lacework of the jib until he crouched, hundreds of feet up, above the wrinkling khaki river. A flock of sunstruck pigeons whirled in harmony around the control house roof.

It was so perfect that he knew he could do it. He stood up, balancing against the breeze, feeling on top of the world. Slowly he raised his hands above his head, cast a glance upwards into the icy sky, then, just before he lost his balance, he chose to rise on tiptoe and launch himself into a taut dive. He tipped off the jib and began to tilt through the sunset.

The sound which came from him was an involuntary shriek of pure joy – he cared neither if he lived nor if he died. His body, pointed like a shuttle, wove a slow circle through the air, hurtling ever downwards to the peaky grey surface. By chance, his dive had him angled perfectly to enter the water with a splashless 'glup' at some dangerously high velocity.

The shock of the water stopping his flight, and of the vicious cold, prevented him from realising immediately that he was still alive. His clothing dragged in the dark water and he started to fight his way upward to the dull light above. Disbelieving and stunned, he gasped as he broke the surface, returning to an almost unchanged peachy evening.

The impetus of his dive still with him, he floundered in his shoes and jacket to the nearest quayside ladder and clambered up the vertical green wall. Once on the quay, he squeezed the edges of his jacket and emptied his shoes. He looked up to the monstrous structure towering above him and scarcely believed that he'd actually dived from yon threadlike piece of lattice-work. Yet he was certainly soaking and he remembered the exhilaration of his descent. He looked around to see if there had been any witnesses to his dive. The docks remained silent and deserted as rust-coloured sunlight flooded the area.

Consequently, when he told anyone he'd dived off the biggest of the dockland cranes into the Clyde, and just for fun, no one believed him.

3 In the first part of the story, there are a number of words describing factual details about the city. For example: *docks, derelict docklands, warehouses.*

Find other words or phrases which describe factual detail about the city. Can you think of a city like this in your country?

4 Look at the first and last sentences of the first part of the story. What do you think happens next?

Now read the second part and find out if you were right.

> So, tonight, he'd told them to come and watch him do it again.
>
> But this time he was afraid. The metal seemed hostile as he hand-over-handed his way up. The evening was still and thundery. He had to get it over. Below, the river lay like sheet steel.
>
> The angle of the jib was changed, but he crawled automatically along the arm until he reached the end. He could barely make out their pinpoint pale faces, upturned. He just wanted to get it over. Careless, he repeated the movements of the first time, toppling headfirst towards the grey below. He felt no inclination to make a sound, not even when he realised there was no reflection expanding to meet him.
>
> His last thought was, 'They'll still never believe me, dammit.'
>
> Two weeks later, a fifteen-foot fence with angled rows of barbed wire at the top prevented further unauthorised access to the crane.

5 There are two important sentences in this part of the story.

The angle of the jib was changed ...
... there was no reflection expanding to meet him.

Write an explanation of what happens and why.

6 Why do you think the man dives from the crane? Why does he do it a second time, and why is he afraid?

7 Sometimes the writer uses some unexpected words and phrases to describe people, things or sensations. What do you usually associate these words with? Use your dictionary if necessary.

creeping   drifting   wrinkling   khaki   taut   wove
peachy   rust-coloured   pinpoint

Now find out what the words and phrases are used to describe in the story. Do you think the images which they create are effective?

8 In Exercises 2 and 5 you wrote some sentences. Look at them again and add any words which are necessary to link the sentences together and make a summary of the story.

Now decide if your summary is missing any details. Think about your answers to Exercises 1, 3 and 6. Would they add anything important to a summary? If necessary, expand your summary, but try to write no more than 150 words in all.

Read your summary again. Check that it reflects what the story says but not how you interpret it.

9 Did you enjoy the story? Can you say why or why not?

Have you ever done anything as dangerous as this for fun? Can you think of anything similar that people might do in your country?

Answer key

Unit 1   Lies

3 The writer approves of telling lies.

4 1 ... you'll be lucky if you ever see your
         stereo again.
     2 ... you're not going to get paid ...
     3 ... the last head of cabbage ... has been
         sitting under the cash register with the cat
         for the last two weeks.
     4 ... you're about to eat an entire family-
         size bag of crisps.
     6 ... the door always falls off like that.
     7 ... you loved the man you dated all
         through university a lot more than you'll
         ever love (your fiancé).

Lie number 5 cannot be matched with a
truth. The truth is probably: ... actually, I
wasn't going to call you. In fact, I hadn't
thought about you for several days.

5 3, 4, 5

6 Suggested answers (of course there are other
interpretations):

Mothers' lies
You want to go somewhere with your
    mother. She doesn't want you to go.
You want to watch a late TV programme.
    Your mother doesn't want you to watch
    it.
At the doctor's: the vaccination probably
    will hurt.
At the dentist's: of course there is reason to
    be afraid.

Fathers' lies
You want your father to play with you. He
    isn't busy but he doesn't want to spend
    time with you.

You ask your father if you can go out. It is
    just as much his affair as your mother's,
    but he doesn't want to decide.
You remind him that he said you could go
    out. He did say it but he has changed his
    mind.

Parents' lies
You've damaged your parents' car. They are
    really very angry.
You can tell them the truth, but beware of
    the consequences.
You can try talking to them about anything,
    but there are some subjects that are
    better avoided.

7 I promise.
    I didn't.
    I did.
    In a minute.
    As soon as this show is over.
    I was going to do it.
    I heard you the first time.
    Why me? It's always me.
    Everybody else has one.
    He hit me first.
    Nobody else's parents make them ...

Unit 2   Coincidences

2 Passage A: Small world
    Passage B: Dreams
    Passage C: Small world
    Passage D: Intuition

3 1 b, 2 b, 3 b, 4 a, 5 a, 6 b

4 A The car that Mr Hudson was in broke
        down twice in four months in the same
        place and for the same reason. Each time
        he was in a different car with a different

driver. The second time he broke down, he saw the man who had been driving the first car on the first occasion drive past him on the motorway.

B Mr Rose dreamt that Fred Kormis, a well-known sculptor whom he had met two years before, had died. Two days later he read the sculptor's obituary in the newspaper.

C Mrs Keary was staying with some friends in London. When she heard someone playing the cello in the flat above, she went upstairs and found a friend she had last seen eight years before. Their friendship was renewed and the woman let Mrs Keary stay in her flat in London.

D Mrs Harper was having dinner with a friend when a strong feeling made her decide to go home early. Her husband had just been taken ill. She was able to get medical help which saved his life.

Unit 3   Nightmare journeys

2 1 negative   4 negative
2 positive   5 negative
3 negative   6 positive

3 'A passenger has been arrested at emigration, and they need to find his bags in the holds before we can fly.'
'We haven't been able to find the bags so we have to offload all the containers and search them. That means that the crew will exceed its maximum hours ...'
'Unfortunately, we haven't yet been able to organise another crew.'
'we have a minor avionics problem'
'the crew's allowable hours of work are once again running out'
'we do seem to have small problem with the electrical system'

4 1 They think he might be a terrorist.
2 The writer is too polite to shout, and therefore does not get a room quickly.
3 He feels he's being treated like a criminal in prison.
4 Experiencing this unfortunate situation together has turned total strangers into good friends.

5 The captain sounded bright when he announced they'd be taking off in five minutes. Now he can't face telling the passengers of yet another delay.
6 It means the plane is about to take off.
7 In other circumstances he would think it rude to draw attention to the driver's incompetence. But on this occasion he complains.

5 Suggested answer:
None of the quotations express exactly what he feels about travelling, but 3 and 5 come close to reflecting his attitude towards his nightmare journey.

Unit 4   The cow that ate the piper

1 Folktales told by storytellers often had a number of different versions until they were written down. They often consisted of an extremely simple storyline or event that was developed and embellished by the storyteller with a lot of extra detail and background colour. This made it not only more enjoyable but also easier to follow, since people were listening rather than reading it.

2 Suggested answer:
The pivotal point is when the servant girl saw the two feet by the fire.

4 Suggested answer:
The storyline is contained in more than half of the sentences. Since the story was told orally, the main function of the extra information is to allow the listener time to digest the storyline. It also provides a lot of background colour.

5 Sentences 3, 5, 6, 8, 10, 11, 12 and 14 summarise the facts. Sentences 4, 7, 9, 13 and 15 interpret the facts.

Unit 5   He was a good lion

2 Statements 1, 3 and 4 are true.

4 *making a scratching and scraping sound with something*: scuffling
giving or sending out: emitting
a deep breath that others can hear: sigh

a well-planned intention: premeditation
draw in air loudly through the nose: sniff
openly unafraid: defiant
a simple song: ditty
a slow run: trot
very quickly: swiftly
a headcovering worn by Muslims, Sikhs and Hindus: turban
aware of what is happening: conscious
surrounded: encompassed

5 1 She was 'a very small girl' – probably about 10 years old.
2 The rules on what to do when confronted by a lion.
3 Probably not, she sings 'a defiant song'.
4 Bishon Singh.
5 No.

7 The writer feels sorry that the lion spent the rest of his life in a cage. She is not angry with him for attacking her.

8 The writer would probably agree with statements 1 and 3.

Unit 6   Bargains

1 The writer would agree with definition 5.

2 a 2, b 6, c 1, d 7, e 5, f 4, g 3

3 1 b, 2 a, 3 a, 4 b

4 1 Toothpaste reduced from £1.20 to £1.15.
2 1p off soap, washing powder or dog food.
3 Clothes they will never wear, furniture they have nowhere to put, roller-skates, pipe-cleaners.
4 The lady who bought a dress, a suitcase and a Persian carpet at reduced prices believed that the money she had saved was money she had made.
5 Half a ton of lamb which won't fit in the freezer, sugar bought in bulk and kept in the lavatory because there was nowhere else to store it.
6 They buy the toothpaste because it is a new product not because it is better than others.

7 A reduction of only 1p is better than no reduction at all.

5 **Suggested answers:**
'To be offered a "gift" of one penny is like being invited to dinner and offered one single pea (tastily cooked), and nothing else.'
'non-smokers will buy pipe-cleaners'
'if she had more time for shopping, she could make a living out of it'
'people rush to buy a freezer just to find out later that it is too small to hold half a ton of New Zealand lamb'
'they bought enough sugar for their lifetime and the lifetime of their children and grandchildren'

Unit 7   A lamp in a window

3 *drunk*: consumed
cautious: wary
driving from side to side: weaving
insults: invectives
crashed: swiped against

6 **Suggested answers:**
'a round pleasant face'
'a cat curled in her lap'
'the cozy room'
'I warmed my hands at the fire'
'a cheerful place occupied by six or seven cats'

8 *bourbon*: whisky
highway: road
catch a ride: get a lift
fix your car: mend your car
transportation: transport
mailman: postman

10 The opinions in brackets are the old lady's. They tell us that she has led an isolated life, and is quite poor. She is intelligent and self-reliant.

12 . . . leading me over to the deep-freeze, and opening it. Inside was nothing but cats: stacks of frozen, perfectly preserved cats – dozens of them. It gave me an odd sensation. 'All my old friends. Gone to rest. It's just that I couldn't bear to lose them. *Completely*.' She

laughed and said: 'I guess you think I'm a bit dotty.'

A bit dotty. Yes, a bit dotty, I thought as I walked under the gray skies in the direction of the highway she had pointed out to me. But radiant: a lamp in a window.

Unit 8   Fun on skis

3 Stories 4 and 1

4 snow   slope   ice   muscle   panic   chair lift   slide   plunge   boot

5 a) '... after a demonstration of the "snow plough" was told to try it out. I did, with my knees carefully together. Unfortunately, the toes of the skis were apart.' (Story 1)
   b) 'We bravely went through the early exercises on small ice slopes until our muscles cried out.' (Story 1)
   'In the icy conditions, I picked up speed.' (Story 1)
   'We queued on an icy patch and I lost my hold on the restraining post. Suddenly out of control, ...' (Story 3)

c) 'I slid forwards between the two skiers who were waiting for the two-man chair to come round the corner behind them.' (Story 3)
   d) 'Not realising the lift didn't stop, he hesitated before attempting to get off, mistiming completely.' (Story 4)
   '... my poor, silly husband went around the wheel of the lift, ...' (Story 4)

6 Story 1: The toes of the skis were apart when the writer tried the snow plough.
Story 2: The writer couldn't sit down and bring the safety bar down in time.
Story 3: The writer lost control while waiting in the queue for the chair lift.
Story 4: The writer's husband hadn't realised that the chair lift wasn't going to stop to let him off.

7 The judges gave the first prize to Story 1.

8 amusing, ridiculous

Unit 9   Loneliness

3 1 young mothers
   2 teenagers
   3 students
   4 celebrities

4 a 3, b 1, c 4, d 2

6

	Sheila	*Lynn*	*George*	*Tony*
Occupation	Housewife	Schoolgirl	Student	Broadcaster
Reasons for loneliness	Left work to have a baby; moved house; knew nobody	Friends don't live near her; no facilities for teenagers; no sport or hobby; shy	Foreigner; arrived at university; didn't understand the British; racism	Works in the media; difficulty making real friends; shy
How they coped with loneliness	Joined National Housewives' Register and goes to regular meetings	Bought a Citizens' Band radio and talks to a lot of people	Went to the Student Advisory Service; became involved in college politics	Has a great job; has one good friend

Unit 10   How would you like to spend the night with him?

1 b   In a newspaper or magazine

3 1 Sentences 2 and 3. It is a poor district in London.
2 Sentences 6, 7 and 8.
3 Vagrancy means having nowhere to live, wandering from place to place with no home, money or job.
4 The answer suggested in the passage is no, a more caring approach is needed.

5 The characteristics of 'community policing':
'an attempt to get close to people again'
'it means focusing our attention on the 90% of people who never commit a crime'
'denying (criminals) opportunities'
'working harder to help their victims'
'being useful to people in every way we can'
'get to know the people'

The advantages:
When the general public trust and respect the police their concern is a powerful weapon against crime and can lead to a drop in the level of street crime.

Unit 11   How well do you travel?

2 The writer would agree with statements 3 and 4.

4 *photographs*: snaps
complaint: grievance
a complete transformation or change: metamorphosis
someone who is not interested in cultural visits: philistine
cigarette: fag
a quick tour: whip-round
madness: lunacy
ridiculous: daft

6 1 You do not know where it is.
2 You want the courier to find your luggage for you.
3 A miserable time alone.
4 A pleasant person to be with.
5 Likely.

Unit 12   Homesickness

2 He was unhappy because he wasn't spending Christmas with his family and friends.

3 1 ... his grandmother had been taken to hospital in Cape Town.
2 ... all the hotels were full.
3 ... he was on his own and he couldn't sleep.
4 ... he had started crying.
5 ... he didn't want to have it on his own.

4 *Springfield*: incredibly beautiful and comfortable
the hotel: fifth class, cracks on the ceiling, dreadful
the hamburger: filthy, greasy, repulsive

His feelings: my morose state, isolated, a really dark and terrible depression, frightful, completely and utterly alone, the most miserable thing ever, in a flood of tears, sorry for myself, alone

People around him: everybody ... was having a family Christmas, a jolly time, laughing and singing, running around on beaches, a great time

The fact that other people were enjoying themselves contrasts sharply with the writer's unhappiness and makes it seem even worse.

5 **Examples:**
completely and *utterly* alone
incredibly alone
terribly Christmas person
incredibly special

The use of these words makes the description of his feelings seem very exaggerated.

6 1 He did not have anything more interesting to do than visit his grandmother.
2 Because the song represented the spirit of Christmas for him.
3 Because everyone was enjoying themselves in the sun and it did not seem like Christmas at all, which in Britain takes place at the coldest time of year.

Unit 13   American dreams decoded

2 Heating in homes and department stores; shopping

3 a) paragraphs 1, 2, 3
   b) paragraphs 4, 5

5 1 Americans like to invert temperatures indoors; they overheat in winter and keep it very cool in summer
   2 'Inside the store it's fractionally more temperate, ...'
   3 The store owners want their image to be one of generosity and so they are over-generous with the heat they provide in their stores.
   4 '... (to have) more – far more – than enough of everything, including food and heat'

6 *General statements*: Americans are fascinated by their own love of shopping. This does not make them unique. It's just that they have more to buy than most other people on the planet. It's also an affirmation of faith in their country, its prosperity and limitless bounty. They have shops the way that lesser countries have statues.
   Example: the rebuilding of the Union Station

   General statements: Shopping is done at the mall. Food stores are among the glories of America.
   Example: the Safeway store in Page, Arizona

7 d

8 They are all very high and convey an idea of great size. Apart from *vast dizzying towers*, they all refer to land features. The writer wants to convey the idea of enormous quantities, so he uses very exaggerated terms. This use of exaggeration in the choice of words reflects the American tendency to exaggerate many other aspects of their way of life.

Unit 14   The aqueduct

2 b

3 **Suggested answer:**
The importance of water, survival at the expense of others, human society

4 They want to know why there is a war, but are ultimately more concerned about the liquid from the aqueduct.
The war in the North supplies the people in the South with liquid for their fields.

5 1 The story is probably set at some time in the past. Words like *aqueduct*, *gargoyle*, *messengers*, *stone baths*, etc. all suggest perhaps the Middle Ages or even earlier. But the sheer size of the population suggests perhaps that the story is set in the future. The effect is that there have always been greed and selfishness in times of war.
   2 The child who says the liquid is red and thick is the only person to question the truth. But the sons in the field are as selfish and cynical as their father is.
   3 It has the effect of referring to an event that is already well-known in the history of the countries involved.
   4 It's an impersonal style, which makes the story even more chilling.
   5 'Soon now the Aqueduct will be finished.'
   'When will the water come?'
   'Bring vases and bowls ...'
   The people gathered by the tens of millions ...
   'It's coming!'
   And from a great distance, there was the sound of rushing and running ...
   It flowed slowly at first and then faster ...
   'It's here! Any second now.'
   6 The one hundred million dead is an extremely high figure. The word *disagree* is a very mild word. This suggests that the cause of the war is not proportionate to its effect.
   7 These words make us realise that the story is an allegory and therefore to be interpreted symbolically.

Unit 15   Traveler

3 1, 4

6 Suggested answers:
1 The son has jet lag after his flight home.
2 He fell asleep suddenly.
3 He experienced something no one else has experienced before.

Other images and similes:
This household has been running a low fever over the trip since weeks before it began …
… though two of the calls were like ship-to-shore communication in which you have to switch from Receive to Send …

7 Suggested answers:
I have never listened to a telephone so intently and with so much pleasure as I did those three times. It was wonderful and moving to hear news from him that was so new to me. In my book, he was the first man to land on the moon …
I sit here amazed. The night when your child returns with dust on his shoes from a country you've never seen is a night you would gladly prolong into a week.

Unit 16   Accidental discoveries

1 Nobel c, Newton a, Pasteur e, Becquerel f, Curie b, Mackintosh d

3 Post-its are self-sticking notes.
They are pieces of sticky paper which can easily be removed.
To temporarily keep Art Fry's place in his choir book.
In offices, on letters and file folders, by telephones and computer screens, in homes on the refrigerator and the TV screen, by the back door.

4 f, j, c, l, i, a, g, e, h, k, b, d

5 made a culture from his own nasal secretions
little practical importance but was a prelude to discovery of penicillin doing research on influenza
carrying out routine laboratory work
concluded that mould was producing something which was deadly to bacteria

6 Suggested answers:
four boys exploring the woods near Montignac
discovered a small hole in the ground
crawled inside
found a narrow passage leading to an underground cave
saw paintings of animals
reported their discovery
expert of prehistoric art said the paintings were authentic
the public were admitted in small groups
after the war, new entrance and better security
visitors now view an exact replica next to original cave
no danger of damaging the original

Unit 17   Love and marriage

2 Their relationship is argumentative and unhappy.

3 Suggested answers:
1 They're having dinner in a restaurant or a hotel.
The man is wearing shorts.
They have a five-year-old child, who complains a lot.
The weather is not very good.

2 *sly* glances: they don't want it to be obvious that they're looking at the other guests
pink-kneed husband: he is faintly ridiculous in his shorts at dinner
complaining pest: the child is as unappealing as its parents
blamed each other: they think the bad weather was the other one's fault

3 'the ghosts of false what-might-have-beens'
'For what neither might have anyway achieved'

4 Their marriage, like the package holiday, looked attractive, but it didn't last long and was disappointing.
'… one written
In the same tempting style; one over which
A watery sun shone the same short while.'

5 Both poems describe a failed marriage in which the partners no longer like each other.

6 1 The son
  2 The parents' voices from the room below
  3 An original loving relationship
  4 The grey coals are compared to the grey-haired, ageing couple, the noise of the coals *hiss* could be the noise of the couple arguing with each other. The original passion (*fire*) they had is now gone from their relationship.

Unit 18   Hospitality

2 A India, B Greece, C Denmark

3 B and C are written from the guest's point of view, A from the host's.

4 1 A last paragraph, 2 B last paragraph, 3 C first paragraph

5 *Unexpected events*:
Passage B: car broke down; villagers arguing about who should put the guest up; prepared a room for the night; mayor's mule pulled car to a garage; old woman made dinner with her own hen; other villagers brought food and drink; made merry until late; brought the repaired car back.
Passage C: no hotel rooms available; a room with strangers; prepared a bath; prepared sandwiches; gave a party.

Similarities:
People offered to take in a stranger who couldn't speak their language, prepared a room for the night, provided food and drink, celebrated with the guest, refused money.

6 **Suggested answers:**
'Hospitality is natural in my village'
'They become a part of the family'
'It is impolite for guests to refuse (food)'
'Hospitality is always disinterested'
'It is a religious act'

Unit 19   Mazes

1 1 d, a rock carving maze; 2 b, a Japanese wooden maze; 3 a, Hampton Court hedge maze. Photo c is the turf maze at Saffron Walden, England.

2 a) large
  b) They have got lost.
  c) Harris

3 *They*: Harris and his cousin
  inside: in the maze
  it: being in the maze
  it: being in the maze
  his: Harris's
  him: Harris

4 Before meeting Harris the people in the maze were fed up, worried and desperate. After meeting Harris they were reassured and relieved.

5 '... because we've walked a good two miles already.'
  '... she wished she never had met Harris ...'
  '... he was an imposter ...'

6 1 Harris didn't know where they were on the map.
  2 In order to find his way back to the entrance, he would need to know whereabouts on the map they were. If he could find the entrance, there would be no need to begin again, because that was where the people wanted to get to.
  3 They had lost confidence in him, and were getting angry. '... the crowd looked dangerous ...' and 'Harris said that he couldn't help feeling that, to a certain extent, he had become unpopular ...'
  4 humorously pleasant
  5 mob
  6 humorous

7   They all got crazy at last, and sang out for the keeper, and the man came and climbed up the ladder outside, and shouted out directions to them. But all their heads were, by this time, in such a confused whirl that they were incapable of grasping anything, and so the man told them to stop where they were, and he would come to them. They huddled together, and waited; and he climbed down, and came in.

He was a young keeper, as luck would have it, and new to the business; and when he got in, he couldn't get to them, and then *he* got lost. They caught sight of him, every now and then, rushing about the other side of the hedge, and he would see them, and rush to get to them, and they would wait there for about five minutes, and then he would reappear again in exactly the same spot, and ask them where they had been.

They had to wait until one of the old keepers came back from his dinner before they got out.

Unit 20   Crane diver

2 The crane diver was a man who climbed up hundreds of feet to the top of a dockland crane overlooking the city, and dived into the water below.

3 crane, towers, churches, cars, expressway, quayside, quay

5 The second time he dived, the angle of the jib was changed, because it was no longer positioned over the water. As he fell there was no reflection expanding to meet him, because he was diving into the ground, not into the river. He killed himself.

7 *creeping*: insects
drifting: smoke
wrinkling: skin
khaki: army uniform
taut: rope
wove: cloth, pattern
peachy: complexion
rust-coloured: metal
pinpoint: accuracy, detail

To the teacher

The primary aim of *Reading 3* is to help the learner develop the skill of reading English. The means of achieving this aim are many, but probably the most important is *learner motivation*. Reading in the mother tongue is such an enjoyable activity that it would seem highly desirable to recreate this enjoyment when the student starts to read in the foreign language. But the motivation to read in the mother tongue may often be different from the motivation to read in the foreign tongue.

The reader in the mother tongue has a reason for reading and the consequent motivation is self-directed. The reason may sometimes be spurious or ephemeral, but at least this reader is in control and can choose what he or she wants to read. But in the foreign language, reading is often a classroom activity, and may be directed and controlled by the teacher. This reader is often told either implicitly or explicitly what to read and how. So how does the teacher in the artificial situation of the classroom recreate the motivation for, and enjoyment of reading that the reader would normally experience in real life?

There seem to be three key factors in stimulating the learner's motivation: the text, the task and the teacher's role. In *Reading 3* we have tried to incorporate these three factors in an attempt to make reading enjoyable and motivating.

The text

The types of text we choose for use in the classroom have an obvious and important role to play in stimulating learner motivation. We have tried to choose material which is varied, interesting and intellectually stimulating to as many people as possible. It does not seem a satisfactory way of promoting motivation to use material which contains familiar ideas and information and in which the only interest is in deciphering the foreign language.

Many of the texts contain some vocabulary which will be unfamiliar to the learner. When we were selecting the texts, it seemed important to us to use as much authentic material as possible, that is to say, material which was not specially written for language learners. We have avoided all carefully graded texts which would pose little or no comprehension difficulties and which would not necessarily develop the learner's reading skills.

Motivation through the text and its content was a primary objective. But realistically, it seems unlikely that a text will interest all of the people all of the time. Another factor seems essential in stimulating motivation: the task.

The task

The tasks or activities which accompany the texts in *Reading 3* have two intentions: the first is to create or maintain learner motivation; the second is to develop the useful microskills for reading.

We have already said that a text and its content will rarely be able to bear the full responsibility for stimulating genuine learner motivation. But if it is accompanied by interesting tasks, we feel that learner motivation can be created and maintained artificially. The classroom context remains artificial and few of the tasks in *Reading 3* could be said to be real-life tasks; we do not usually have to match headings, pictures and paragraphs, or unscramble sentences when we read a novel or a magazine! Yet these kinds of tasks may be problem-solving activities or stimuli for discussion. They are not always linguistically complex, but are often conceptually difficult, and therefore enjoyable and motivating in their own right.

The microskills for reading which are presented in *Reading 3* are developed using a variety of different activity types.

Extracting main ideas It is important to help the learner look for the main ideas of a passage and to avoid getting distracted by unfamiliar vocabulary. Typical activity types which develop this skill are matching exercises; text with picture, text with heading, etc. Sometimes, there may be an extra sentence, or an extra picture. This only makes the reader think a bit more!

Inferring A writer may want you to understand more than the actual words you read. Inferring activities draw the readers' attention to the overall atmosphere of the passage. They also help build their vocabulary.

Predicting Before learners read a text, it may be helpful to encourage them to look at the subject or the title of the passage, and to think about the possible content. But remember: it doesn't matter if the learners do not predict correctly. The activity still helps prepare them for reading.

Dealing with unfamiliar words In this book there will be many words which the learner will not understand. This is because all the passages are examples of real-life written English. It is important to try and guess the general sense of a difficult word, and there are a number of activities which help the reader deal with unfamiliar vocabulary without using dictionaries or asking the teacher to explain or translate.

Reading for specific information We sometimes read to find the answer to a particular question, and not to understand the general sense of the passage. There are a number of exercises like this to help the learner read for specific information.

Linking ideas   Often a writer uses several different words to describe the same idea. Sometimes the use of a pronoun, for example, may be confusing, although the context usually makes the meaning clear. This type of exercise concentrates on the words used to link ideas.

Evaluating the text   In order to understand a text more thoroughly, the reader may need to appreciate the writer's viewpoint and the reason it was written, as well as to distinguish between facts and opinions. The exercises which develop this particular microskill help to develop the learner's more critical faculties.

Understanding the writer's style   At this level, it begins to be more important and enjoyable for the reader to appreciate the reason why the writer uses certain words and expressions, and the effect they create. The reader's attention is drawn to a number of stylistic devices such as exaggeration, humour and imagery.

Reacting to the text   In order to engage the readers' interest in a text, it is useful to encourage them to react in a more subjective way to, for example, its humour or its literary and poetic appeal. The readers' reactions to other text types, such as instructions, may be registered by them carrying out the instructions and demonstrating their comprehension in a non-verbal way. This skill may also develop their ability to supply missing context and information about the text.

However, it has to be said that one disadvantage of giving too much importance to microskills is that the learner may already have acquired some or all of them. In this case, they should be seen as devices for motivating the learner.

The teacher's role

Motivation is a most elusive factor in learning: we know it facilitates learning, but we don't quite know how to stimulate it, even though we all know for sure when we are addressing motivated learners. Our attempt in *Reading 3* has been to use as many different texts and tasks as possible to achieve this. But ultimately, the teacher has the final responsibility in making sure the learner remains happy and interested in his or her work by being flexible about the teaching material to be used. As a teacher using *Reading 3*, you can:

- either work through each unit in order or choose only those which are likely to interest your students. You may not have time to do every unit, and not every unit will interest everyone.
- either do every exercise, or only do those which are useful or interesting to the students.
- either start at the beginning of the book and work through to the end, or choose to do units in random order. There is no particular grading in the book, although the texts at the beginning tend to be linguistically less complex than those at the end.

– let the students work alone, or in pairs.
– let the students choose the texts which interest them, or direct them to particular units.
– choose units which cover language points or themes that are related to the main syllabus of your course.
– extend the work covered in the unit with further discussion or writing practice.
– help learners to read actively if you avoid translating or explaining every single item of vocabulary which they do not understand.

Finally, remember that this book is designed to help you teach, and to help your learners learn. It is a framework for reading practice, and not a straitjacket. Don't hesitate to adapt the material if you so choose. We hope you and your students enjoy using *Reading 3*.

Acknowledgements

The authors and publishers are grateful to the authors, publishers and others who have given permission for the use of copyright material identified in the text. It has not been possible to identify the sources of all the material used and in some cases the publishers would welcome information from copyright owners.

Collins, Angus & Robertson of HarperCollins Publishers Australia for the extracts on pp. 2–4 from *Great Lies* by Jo Donnelly; HarperCollins Publishers for the extract on p. 5 from *Collins COBUILD Dictionary* and for the poems on pp. 63 and 65 'The Package', 'I Caught a Train That Passed the Town Where You Lived' and 'The Cynic's only Love Poem' from *Storm Damage* by Brian Patten, published by Unwin Hyman of HarperCollins Publishers; *The Observer* for the extracts on p. 6 on 'Coincidences' from *The Observer Review*, for the stories on p. 31 entitled 'Funniest moment on skis', and for the extracts on pp. 49–50 from 'American Dreams Decoded' from *The Sunday Observer*; MacQuitty International Collection for the top photograph on p. 8; Venice Simplon-Orient-Express for the bottom photograph on p. 8; Longman Group UK Ltd for quotations 1, 2 and 4 on p. 9, from *Contradictory Quotations*; Richard Scott Simon for quotations 3, 5 and 6 on p. 9, from *The Penguin Dictionary of Humorous Quotations* by Fred Metcalf, published by Penguin Books; *The Independent* for the extract on p. 11 'Hong Kong high jinx' by James Long, and for the extract on p. 46 'Worst of Times – Dai Llewellyn' by Danny Danziger; Hulton-Deutsch Collection for the photograph on p. 12 by William Grundy, 1857; The University of Chicago Press for the folktale on p. 13 entitled 'The Cow that ate the Piper' from *Folktales of Ireland*, edited and translated by Sean O'Sullivan; The J. Allan Cash Photolibrary for the photographs on pp. 16, 21 and 69 (d); André Deutsch Ltd for the extract on pp. 22–3 from *How to be Poor* by George Mikes (published 1983); Hamish Hamilton Ltd and Random House Inc. for the short story on pp. 25–9 and 79–80 entitled 'A Lamp in a Window' from *A Capote Reader* by Truman Capote, copyright © 1987 by Alan U. Schwarz, reprinted by permission of Random House Inc.; Times Newspapers Ltd for the extracts on pp. 34–6 from 'The Loneliness Report' by John Nicholson and Jill Eckersley in *The Sunday Times Magazine* 11.12.83, © Times Newspapers Ltd 1983 and for the extracts on pp. 41–3 from 'Holidays: Pleasure or packaged ordeal?' by David Wickers in *The Sunday Times* 5.4.87, © Times Newspapers Ltd 1987; Collett Dickenson & Pearce for the photograph on p. 37; The Metropolitan Police Service for the recruitment advertisement on pp. 38–40; Don Congdon Associates Inc. for the short story on p. 53 'The Aqueduct' by Ray Bradbury; Ellen Levine Literary Agency Inc. and Faber & Faber Ltd for the article 'Traveler' by Garrison Keillor on pp. 55–7, reprinted by permission of Garrison Keillor from *We are still married* (Viking Penguin, 1989), copyright © by Garrison Keillor; John Wiley & Sons Inc. for the extracts on pp. 60–2 from *Serendipity: Accidental Discoveries in Science* by Royston M. Roberts; Rogers, Coleridge & White Ltd for the poem 'The Son' on p. 64, from *The Well-Wishers* by Edward Lucie-Smith, published by Oxford University Press, 1974; Robert Harding Picture Library for the photograph on p. 66; *The Unesco Courier* for the extracts on pp. 66–8 on 'Hospitality', reprinted from *The Unesco Courier*, February 1990 ('Krupa Sindku and the Beggar' by Prafulla Mohanti, 'Where foreigner means guest' by André Kedros, 'A desire to receive guests' by Georges Lisowski); Historic Royal Palaces Photographic Library, Hampton Court Palace, for photograph (a) on p. 69, British Crown Copyright, Historic Royal Palaces; The John Hillelson Agency Ltd for photographs (b) and (c) on p. 69, by Dr Georg Gerster; Valerie Thornton for the photograph on p. 73 and the short story 'Crane Diver' on pp. 74–5, from *Streets of Gold* edited by Moira Burgess and Hamish Whyte, published by Mainstream Publishing Co. (Edinburgh) Ltd.

The short story on pp. 17–18 and 20 entitled 'He was a Good Lion' from *West with the Night* by Beryl Markham was published by North Point Press.

Drawings by Julie Anderson, Peter Brown, Ian Dicks, Leslie Marshall and Chris Rothero.

Book designed by Peter Ducker MSTD.